He is no Fool

Jim Elliot

He is no Fool

Jim Elliot

Irene Howat

CHRISTIAN FOCUS

For Anna

Copyright © 2005 Christian Focus Publications
ISBN 1-84550-064-4
Published by
Christian Focus Publications
Geanies House, Fearn, Tain, Ross-shire
IV20 1TW, Scotland
United Kingdom
www.christianfocus.com
email: info@ christianfocus.com

Cover design by J Sherlock
Cover illustration Neil Reed
Printed and bound in Denmark
by Nørhaven Paperback A/S

Contents

Aeroplanes and Bridges

Jim looked at the kitchen table and saw in his mind a completed model Spitfire. His sister, Jane, looked at the table and saw dozens of bits and pieces, none of which made much sense to her. Maybe that's because she was just seven years old, while Jim was all of 13. When their mother, Clara Elliot, looked at the kitchen table, she saw a tidying up job that needed done by bedtime.

'May I begin making my new model tonight?' Jim asked, knowing the answer very well, but ever hopeful.

Mrs Elliot grinned. 'If I said "yes", I'd have to prise you away with a grappling iron to get you to bed. Best wait until tomorrow when your mind is fresh anyway.'

Bert laughed. 'His mind is fresh 24 hours a day when it's focused on aeroplanes or sailing ships. But I don't see him begging for a late night to do schoolwork.'

Bert, who was the second of the four Elliot children, and three years older than Jim, thought he was really quite grown up. Despite that, he was as excited as his little brother about the Spitfire. After all, it was the latest thing in aviation, and he reckoned that it would win the war against the Germans. The oldest of the family, Bob, who wasn't at home that night, would have enjoyed helping build the aeroplane too. But even to Bob, who was 19, Mum Elliot's word was law. If she said the model had to be packed away till tomorrow, that's just what happened. And it usually happened without a grumbling match, because all their lives the Elliot children had known that Dad and Mum only said 'no' when they really meant it. Arguing about it made so little difference that the youngsters gave it up early on.

Mum Elliot was strict, but she wasn't unreasonable. She knew that Jim was taking his time packing up the pieces because he didn't want to lose any of the littlest ones.

'Those wings are very fragile looking,' she said, as she watched.

Jim's eyes lit up. Here was an opportunity to talk on one of his favourite subjects.

'Yes,' he agreed. 'The Spitfire is quite different from the usual fat-winged monoplanes or biplanes. It has a really large root chord that makes the wings very strong even though they're thin. And do you know what?' he asked, but didn't wait for a reply. 'Each of the Spitfire's wings houses eight Colt/Browning .303 machine guns! I guess that's why it's called the Spitfire. It can swoop down from the sky spitting fire on its target as it dives.'

Jim's mother was just about to ask for more details about the aeroplane, when she caught her son's eye and realised that if she asked just one more question, they'd still be sitting side by side at the table at midnight. Once the boy started on a subject, there was no stopping him.

'Enough!' Mum Elliot laughed. And the pair of them joined the rest of the family at the fireside.

Dad had the Bible open already, and the reading was about heaven and how wonderful it would be. Jim listened to his father reading, and followed the words in his mind.

10

They were wonderful words. He'd heard them so often, and read them over and over again. So when his father reached verse four, Jim was able to join in and say the words along with him. 'He will wipe away every tear from their eyes. There will be no more death or mourning or crying or pain, for the old order of things has passed away.'

The Elliot young people couldn't remember a time when their day had not begun with a reading from the Bible and prayer, and they couldn't remember a night when it hadn't ended in just the same way.

When Jim went to bed at night, he tried to keep the evening Bible reading in his mind. He liked when that was the last thing he thought about before falling asleep. But tonight his mind was all of a jumble. He could picture Spitfires dodging and diving through the air, spitting their deadly fire on the enemy below. And they were all muddled up with thoughts about heaven, where there was to be no tears, no death or mourning, no crying or pain. He thought about Europe, in the throes of the Second World War, with bombs maybe dropping on London or Berlin as he lay comfortably in bed. Jim rolled over and tried to snuggle his mind as well as his body deep in the blankets. But thoughts of war and of heaven would not go away.

'It's a shame that these planes are made to kill people,' he decided, just as sleep crept up on him. 'It would be great if they could be used to help people rather than to shoot them.'

Bert crept into the room to get ready for bed, and was surprised that his little brother was already asleep.

'I don't know how he does it,' thought Bert. 'I think he must have an on/off switch!'

Early the following evening, Spitfire building began in earnest. Jane was trusted to sort the pieces out by shape, while Jim and Bert consulted the instruction sheet.

'Doesn't the stressed skin wing cover make it easily damaged?' Jim asked his brother.

'Yes, it does,' agreed Bert. 'The Hurricane is a much stronger plane, but it's not nearly so versatile. The Spitfire is the nippiest of all. The one thing that it can't do is nose over into a dive without the engine coughing. The Germans are one up on us there. Their Messerschmitt Bf-109s can roll right over without cutting out. Spitfire pilots can only half-roll before diving.'

'Why does that happen?' asked Jim.

'I guess it has something to do with the carburetted Rolls-Royce Merlin engine,' Bert suggested. 'And the thing about war is that there's no time to make refinements on planes. You just have to keep producing them to maintain the forces in the air.'

As Bert spoke, Jim remembered his falling asleep thoughts.

'Wouldn't it be great if aircraft could be used for helping people rather than fighting?' he asked.

'Some are,' Bert reminded him. 'Look at the Northrop Alpha. It carries up to 465 lbs of mail.'

Jim grinned. 'I'd like to fly one of them. Sitting in an open cockpit really appeals to me!'

Bert shivered. 'Actually, I quite like the thought of a Beech Staggerwing.'

'Model C17L?' asked his younger brother. 'You're into real luxury class travel there. I'll stick with the Northrop Alpha and its open cockpit. And I'll wave to you as I buzz past!'

Jane, who wished she knew enough about aircraft to join in her big brothers' conversation, grabbed the chance. There was one plane she did know about, and Jim talking of buzzing past reminded her of it.

'My favourite plane is the Granville Gee Bee,' she chipped in. 'Because it's the same shape as a bumble bee.'

'Quite right!' laughed Jim. 'But it can fly at speeds up to 252 mph, which makes it faster than any bumble bee I've ever seen.'

His little sister stored that piece of information carefully in her memory. There was no telling when it would come in useful in the future. Being the only girl in the family made Jane collect useful snippets of technical information that she could toss into conversations with her brothers' friends. Sometimes that really surprised them!

Interesting things appealed to Jim Elliot. And the history of Portland in Oregon, to which his family had moved from Seattle before he was born, interested him very much indeed.

'Your Portland assignments should be completed before the summer holidays,' his class teacher said, towards the end of April 1940. You can take your time researching them. Choose what aspect of the city most interests you from the list I've given you.'

'I'd like to write about the bridges over the Willamette River,' DK told Jim, as they walked from the school to the bicycle racks. 'You could help me with my research. You're good with facts and figures.'

'I wouldn't mind visiting some of the bridges with you, if that's what you mean,' agreed Jim. 'But I can't decide what aspect of the city I'd like to write on.'

'Portland's geography is interesting,' he thought, as he freewheeled down a hill on his way home from school. 'Although it's a big port city, it's not actually on the coast. But when the Willamette and Columbia rivers meet, there is such a volume of water that it's as good as being on the Pacific Coast. Even huge ocean-going ships steam up-river to Portland, bringing a great variety of things in their holds.'

His brothers had taken Jim to see ships' cargoes being unloaded. Jim could list all the main imports, because he'd had to learn them as a little boy at school. 'Lumber and furniture, wheat and flour, canned and fresh fruits to sell; packed meat, paper and paper pulp, chemicals and wool as well.' Jim laughed aloud. 'If that's meant to be poetry, it's awful! I suppose it was made to rhyme to help us remember it.'

The following Saturday, DK and Jim set out on their bikes to look at some of the city's bridges.

'Which is the oldest one?' DK asked.

'The Hawthorn is the oldest highway bridge over the Willamette. It was built in 1910. But the one I like best is the Steel Bridge that was built two years later. Its two spans can be raised and lowered independently of each other.'

'My favourite is St John's Bridge,' DK said. 'It's the only steel suspension bridge in Portland. When the setting sun hits the bridge, it looks as though it's on fire.'

'I remember Bob and Bert taking me to see it when it opened. I think I was about four at the time,' Jim commented.

'That's right,' agreed DK. 'It opened in 1931. And the Burnside Bridge was built five or so years before that.'

'Portland's bridges would make an interesting assignment,' Jim thought aloud.

'That's why I got there first!' laughed DK. 'You'll have to think of something else.'

'I am,' agreed Jim. 'I'm thinking it's time for our picnic. I'm starving.'

The boys found a grassy patch within sight of St John's Bridge, and they discussed its streamlined design as they ate their way through the egg sandwiches Mum Elliot had provided.

Quarter of an hour later, both boys were comfortably full, comfortably warm and more than a little sleepy. They lay on the grass and talked for a while.

'I think Jesus is rather like a bridge,' Jim said, looking up into the bright blue afternoon sky.

'Don't see it myself,' grinned DK. 'But nearly everything reminds you about Jesus. The only thing that reminds me about him is once a month when I'm hauled out of a perfectly good long lie to go to church.'

Jim didn't say anything aloud, but he did say a silent prayer for his friend.

'OK then,' said DK. 'Explain yourself. How come Jesus is like a bridge?'

Sitting up, Jim wondered how to explain what he was thinking.

'It's like this,' he said, 'when God made Adam and Eve, he made everything perfect. And the Bible says that God used to walk with them in the Garden of Eden. Then it all went pear-shaped when Adam and Eve sinned. Since then there has been a chasm between God and man, the chasm of sin.'

'You've preached your sermon without mentioning a bridge!' laughed DK. 'But I suppose it's still to come.'

'And it's coming right now,' Jim agreed. 'When Jesus died on the cross, it was so that those who trust in him, and ask him to forgive their sins, could have their sins forgiven. He opened the way back to God. Jesus is like a bridge that allows all who trust in him to cross over the chasm of sin and go to heaven when they die.'

DK looked at St John's Bridge.

'You mean it's as though the only way over the Willamette River was by one bridge, and only those who crossed it could get to the other side. And the one way to get from earth to heaven is by believing in Jesus, who is therefore like a bridge between man and God.'

'That's an even better sermon than mine,' Jim smiled.

DK looked surprised. 'I'm not a preacher-man,' he said. 'And I guess I never will be.'

'Have you always been religious?' asked DK, as the pair of them cycled for home.

'What do you mean?' wondered Jim. 'I don't know if I am religious.'

'That bit about putting your trust in Jesus. Have you done that?' queried DK.

'Yes, I have,' Jim said, trying not to sound too excited.

He had prayed that he'd have the opportunity to tell DK about the Lord, but usually his friend wasn't interested.

'Want to hear about it?' asked Jim casually.

'Suppose I might as well,' his friend said. 'But don't preach at me. I was at church a week ago Sunday, and I'm not due another sermon for a full two-and-a-half weeks.'

'In a way I've always believed in Jesus,' Jim said, as he freewheeled down a slope. 'Dad and Mum are Christians, and I've always known they loved the Lord with all their hearts. You only need to be in our home for a day to know that.'

'Yea, they're different,' agreed DK. 'But I want to hear about you, not about Dad and Mum Elliot…'

Jim explained how the Bible was read in his home morning and evening each day, and always had been. He told DK that his parents prayed for them and prayed with them every single day, and how he and his brothers and sister had heard stories of Jesus since before they could remember.

'One night, when I was six,' Jim said, 'we'd all been at a meeting …'

'You mean a church service?' asked his pal.

'Yea, kind of,' agreed Jim. 'And I knew in my heart that night that I really, truly trusted the Lord Jesus Christ as my Saviour. I remember telling Mum that the Lord Jesus could come wherever he wanted because all our family were now Christians, apart from Jane, who was still too young to know him.'

'What do you mean the Lord Jesus could come whenever he wanted. He came 2000 years ago!'

'But he's coming back one day,' Jim said. 'And when he does, he'll take all who believe in him to heaven.'

'And the rest?' asked DK.

'Those who don't go to heaven, go to hell,' Jim said seriously. 'And I'm not making that up. It's in the Bible.'

The boys cycled in silence for a while. For the first time DK was giving some thought to the Christian faith. And Jim? He was praying for his friend.

Family Roots and Vegetable Shoots

The weeks until the school summer holiday passed quickly. At least, they did until there was just a fortnight to go. That was when Jim started counting the days until the family were due to go to Eastern Washington on holiday to their grandparents. But the thing about counting the days is that it makes time move more slowly!

At night Jim lay in bed thinking of the rolling hills stretching from his grandfather's house away to Mt Adams in the distance. He pictured the purple haze that capped Mt Adams in the evening, and the glow on it when the morning sun shone. Whenever he thought about the Luginbuhl homestead, he could smell it as well as see it in his mind. There was the smell of peaches warm in the sun and of hot bread fresh from the oven. Then there was the smell of young lambs and of newly picked broad beans. It seemed to Jim Elliot that he could walk the length and breadth of the Luginbuhl homestead with his eyes shut, just following the smells of summer all along the way.

Although the clock in the family kitchen seemed to grind almost to a halt the last two days of term, the school holiday came at last. And it no sooner arrived than the Elliots took themselves off for their much longed-for holiday in Eastern Washington. The journey was never boring as there was so much to see. In any case, Jim hadn't learned to be bored as there always seemed to be interesting things to think about even in those very occasional moments where there was nothing to do.

'Goodness me!' Grandmother Luginbuhl laughed, when she saw Jane. 'It feels like I only turned my back and you've gone and grown!'

Jim was next in line to receive her attention. 'Well, young man, you've sprouted up too!' she smiled. 'I think your grandfather has a busy summer planned for you.'

As his brothers were welcomed, Jim wondered what his grandmother meant. Grandfather was always busy, though he was never so busy that Jim felt he needed to get out of the way.

'May I walk round the meadow?' Jim asked, looking at the field of sheep in the distance.

'Of course you can,' Grandmother Luginbuhl laughed. 'And I expect you'll be well remembered.'

Jim grinned. Even if the rest of the family didn't know what she meant, Jim certainly did. As he approached the meadow, he realised that he had grown since last summer, and he reckoned he could probably manage to gate-vault over rather than open the gate and go through. He ran the last few yards, put his left hand on the top bar of the gate, swung his legs up and over to the right, and landed in one piece and in the right direction on the other side. Looking quickly round to see if anyone was watching – and nobody was – Jim tucked his new trick away and decided to produce it to maximum effect one day in front of his brothers. Until now, they had been able to gate-vault and he had not.

'Hello there,' said Jim, to the first sheep that looked up at him.

She had plenty of grass to keep her busy, and soon

lowered her head and got on with the day's work of eating. Several other sheep raised their heads and looked at the newcomer. 'Hi,' he said to some of them. 'How're you doing?' he asked others. All alike looked up at the stranger, decided that having their dinner was more interesting, and looked down again. But not quite all. One sheep kept looking, and then she turned in Jim's direction and walked towards him. The boy grinned as the sheep picked up speed. He plonked himself down on the grass just in time for the sheep to nudge against him in welcome.

'So you remember me, old girl,' he laughed. 'And if Grandmother thinks I've grown, it's nothing to how much bigger you are!'

He lay down in the meadow grass and remembered the previous year. They had been on holiday at the homestead at lambing time, and he had bottle-fed an orphan lamb, that seemed to have grown up into a fine figure of a sheep.

'Grandfather said I spent too much time with you and nearly turned you into a pet lamb,' he told the sheep, who seemed to know she was being spoken to, for she head-butted him in reply.

'And he wasn't best pleased, because he once had a lamb that was so tame that she tried to go into the house, even when she was grown into a big smelly sheep.'

Another head-butting followed. 'Sorry old girl,' the lad laughed. 'I wasn't being personal!'

Leaving the sheep behind, Jim started running in order to vault over the gate once again, but he caught sight of Bert just on time.

'Whoa!' he whistled through his teeth. 'I don't want him to see me do it yet.'

Walking sedately to the gate, Jim unlatched it, walked

through, closed the gate behind him and strolled to join his brother.

'Good to be back?' Bert asked.

His young brother nodded. 'Yea,' he agreed. 'It's always good to be back.'

That evening, when all the day's work was done, the family gathered round the big wooden table in the kitchen. The talk was all about family things, and about what had happened since they were last together. It was a warm evening, and Jane, who was tired from a combination of excitement, the journey, and newly baked bread, nearly fell asleep at the table. When she woke with a start, Mum Elliot suggested it was very nearly time for bed.

'May I have an olden-days story first, please?' she asked.

'Which one would that be?' enquired Grandmother, pretty sure she knew the answer. And she was right.

'The one about how you and Grandfather came here,' the girl suggested. 'I think it's a lovely story.'

Grandfather grinned. 'So do I,' he agreed. 'Now, where does that story begin?'

Bob, Bert, Jim and Jane could all have told him where the story began, but nobody said a word. It would have spoiled their annual reminder of their history.

'As you know, I was brought up in Berne in Switzerland,' Grandfather began, in the accent the children so much loved. 'And when I was a young man I left Berne for the great United States of America. I had enough money to get me as far as Colorado, so that's where my travels ended. For a while I worked there in a smelter, saving some of every dollar I earned. And when I had saved enough, I moved

22

over here to Washington and bought myself a homestead.'

Jane was wide awake now. She and her brothers knew the story well, but they still didn't want to miss any of it.

'Not too long afterwards, I heard that a young woman who used to sing with me in the choir in Berne had also reached America. Now, that was good news,' he smiled, 'because I liked her a lot. She was the daughter of a ribbon-maker, and a fine young woman. I wrote to her and eventually persuaded her to come to Washington. And the rest, as they say, is history. The young woman is not so young now,' he grinned at his wife. 'But I'm glad the ribbon-maker's daughter married me. For, if she had not, none of you would be here. And that would be a pity.'

Turning her attention to her mother, Jane said, 'Tell us how you and Dad met.'

'OK,' Mum said, 'but that won't take long.'

She set the rocking chair swaying gently backward and forward, backward and forward, and began her story in time with the movement of the chair.

Back – 'Your grandparents brought up two children in the homestead, your Uncle Jim and me.'

Forward – 'When I was 18, I went to a public meeting to hear a Mr Ironside preaching.'

Back – 'But Mr Ironside didn't come alone; there was a young man called Fred Elliot with him.'

The chair went forward and back as she sat smiling at the memory.

'Three years later, when I was a student, I went along to a week of meetings at which young Fred Elliot was speaking,' she continued.

'When Dad saw you sitting in the audience the first

night, he thought what a pretty girl you were,' Bert chipped in. 'But as you had a young man by your side, there was no point in him thinking any further.'

Mum Elliot's chair swung forward – 'But I confused him well and truly...' she laughed.

The chair swung backwards - '... for I had a different young man by my side the next night, and a different one again the following night!'

She drew the rocker to a halt, 'And do you know what?'

Jane did know. 'Dad asked if he could walk you home one night.'

'And two years later, in 1918, we were married,' Mum Elliot concluded. 'Which brings us right up to bedtime, or you'll not be fit to get up in the morning to help.'

After the young folk were in bed, Grandfather and Grandmother Luginbuhl and Mum Elliot sat and talked.

'How are the young folk doing?' Grandfather asked.

Mum Elliot gave a run-down of what they were up to, especially their interest in the Bible and in what was happening in church.

Grandmother closed her eyes in thought. 'I remember Jim, when he was just six years old, standing up on the garden swing to preach to his young friends.'

'Is he still telling people about Jesus?' Grandfather asked.

Mum Elliot was able to reassure her father that young Jim was still as enthusiastic about his faith in Jesus as he had ever been.

'People say that we are forcing religion down the children's throats,' Mum Elliot said sadly. 'They don't seem to understand that we want the very best for them, and there is none better than Jesus. They'll never find a better friend in all their lives than the Lord Jesus Christ.'

Her parents nodded in agreement.

'One father told me that he hoped his son would be healthy and wealthy when he grew up,' Mum Elliot said. 'He thought I was off my head when I said I'd like our children to be healthy, if that's God's will, but I'm not at all sure that I'd like them to be wealthy. Money brings temptations with it. I think it's maybe better to have just enough money than too much.'

'Money can be a real curse,' Grandfather said. 'I've seen so many promising young people lose their heads when they had $10 in their pockets.'

The young Elliots spent the next few days reacquainting themselves with the land around the homestead. Each year it was almost the same, but Grandfather always had some new things growing on a trial bed somewhere.

'Have you been in the orchard yet?' he asked Jim, early one morning. 'Or would you like to walk it with me after breakfast?'

'I've had a look round, but I'd love to walk it with you.'

Most mornings either Grandfather or Grandmother walked the orchard, checking on the new fruits that were just beginning to grow.

Jim felt really quite grown up as he and the old man tramped between the trees.

'You look that side for any fruits that are growing in a tight bunch,' he told the lad, as they went between two rows of plum trees. 'And if you do see any, pluck one or two of the fruits out.'

'Is that to let the air in and stop mould growing?' Jim

asked, remembering from the previous summer.

'It is indeed. And here's a bag to put them in. There's no point in pulling off mouldy fruits and dropping them on the grass for the mould to spread from there…'

They walked along in companionable silence, Jim picking out occasional fruits, and his grandfather doing the same.

They turned at the bottom of the orchard into a short avenue of peach trees.

'I know what we're looking for here,' said Jim.

'And what would that be?'

'We're looking for leaves that have curled round on themselves. It's called peach-leaf curl,' he said, dredging up the name from the bottom of his memory.

'Well, my lad,' laughed Grandfather, 'you've not forgotten about God's good creation while you've been doing all that book-learning in Portland, Oregon!'

It was lunchtime when grandfather and grandson returned to the house, and both were mightily pleased with how the morning had gone. Grandfather was pleased at how interested Jim was in growing things, and Jim was pleased to have had the old man to himself. He'd told him all about DK and his bridge assignment, and about how he had explained to his school friend that Jesus was like a bridge to heaven, the only bridge that can take anyone from earth to heaven.

'What did you do your assignment on?' Grandfather asked, as they rested for a while before starting on the afternoon's work.

Jim grinned. 'I did it on the financial history of Portland.'

The old man looked sidelong at the lad. 'Finance?' he

thought. 'That doesn't sound like Jim's kind of thing.'

'You see,' the boy explained. 'The financial history of Portland is really one big adventure after another. Just five years after the city was laid out, the Californian gold rush was in full swing, and Portland became a supply point for the goldfields. That had hardly died down when the railroad came to Oregon. Then towards the end of the 19th Century it was gold all over again, only then the city made its money from supplying gold minefields in Alaska.'

'That does sound as though it could be interesting,' the old man agreed. 'But I don't think it would have been the subject I'd have chosen.'

'Nor me,' laughed Jim. 'But when I should have been choosing the topic for my assignment I was too busy building a model Spitfire, and I had to take the only topic that was left!'

Jim and his grandfather spent that afternoon finding small twiggy branches that had fallen off the trees around the homestead and using them to stake along some rows of young peas.

'Don't put them right beside the pea shoots,' Grandfather said. 'Push them into the ground a couple of inches away, then you'll not damage the roots. The wind blows the pea plants around enough that they'll find the branches in a day or two.'

As Jim pushed a branch in the earth two inches from a small pea plant, he looked at it and smiled. 'The tendrils are already curling round each other,' he said. 'As soon as they head in the right direction for the branch, they'll catch on and wrap themselves round it in no time. Will there be peas to eat before we leave?'

'Not from this lot,' Grandfather said. 'But round in the back garden, in the shelter of the high fence, I've a new early variety growing. It's called Jim's Special.'

The boy looked at his grandfather and didn't know whether he was being serious or not.

'Scrub your hands thoroughly,' Grandmother said, 'or there's no supper for either of you.'

Grandfather and Jim looked at each other and smiled.

'It's good clean soil,' the old man laughed. 'And there'd be very little for supper if I didn't get my hands dirty every day.'

As they ate their home-grown salad greens with home produced eggs and home-cured ham, Jim thought about the day.

'I'd rather get my hands dirty staking peas here in Washington then scrabbling around for gold dust in the glaring Californian sun.'

'And so say all of us,' Fred laughed. 'There are few places better in the world than right here where the family belongs.'

'We're really country folk on both sides of the family, aren't we?' asked Jane.

'You certainly are,' Mum Elliot agreed. 'While I was being brought up here among all the wonderful things your grandfather grows, Dad was raised surrounded by grazing land. Grandfather Elliot's stock-trading still keeps him busy. And in the summer, when the stock looked after itself, Dad was out in the fields getting his hands dirty too.'

Grandmother Luginbuhl came in right at the end of that conversation and just caught the final words.

'Are your hands still dirty, young man?' she said, taking Jim by the wrist and examining them.

She couldn't work out why everyone burst out laughing, but that didn't matter. Grandmother Luginbuhl joined in anyway.

The Stamp Man

'We're having missionaries staying with us for a few days,' Mum Elliot told her family, soon after they'd returned from their holiday at the Luginbuhl homestead. 'They were meant to be staying with another family, but that arrangement has fallen through.'

'I guess that means I'm out of my bed,' Jim said.

His brother grinned. 'You're not the only one.'

The Elliot young folk were well used to giving up their beds for visitors, as their parents seemed to be always asking people to stay with them.

'Will the missionaries bring their children?' Jane asked, hopefully.

'I'm afraid their children are all grown up,' replied Mum.

'Does that mean they are very old?' the girl wondered.

Mum shrugged her shoulders. 'They are older than we are,' she admitted. 'But I know you'll find them interesting. They live an amazing life.'

'Tell me about it,' suggested Jane.

'That I will not do,' laughed Mum Elliot. 'They can tell you about it themselves.'

Tidying his room was a bit of a problem to Jim. It wasn't that he was untidy, far from it, it was just that he had so many collections of things and so many models he had built that space was rather limited. However, he did his best, and the room was soon ready for their guests.

'I'll go and pick some flowers for their room,' Jim said, taking the kitchen scissors out the drawer.

Five minutes later, he was back with a mixed bunch of flowers, but all of them in shades of blue.

'What lovely flowers,' his mum said. 'You really do have an artist's eye.'

Jim grinned. It wasn't the first time he'd been told that.

They were just clearing up after their afternoon tea when their guests arrived. It was Mr Armstrong's eyes that Jim noticed first.

'They sparkle like diamonds,' he thought. 'And he looks as though he laughs a lot.'

Jane had already decided that Mrs Armstrong was one of the cheeriest women she had ever seen. Although her face was covered in lines, they were in all the right places. There were laughter lines around her mouth and happy smiley lines to the sides of both her eyes. 'Yes,' thought Jane. 'Mrs Armstrong and I are going to be good friends.'

When the Armstrongs were shown to the room they were going to sleep in, they went off to unpack. Mrs Armstrong was back quite soon, and she apologised that her husband would be a little while.

'Is he all right?' Mum Elliot asked.

Mrs Armstrong winked at Jane. 'Let's just say that although he's an elderly man, he hasn't quite grown up yet.'

Jim looked at his mother, and both wondered what on earth their guest could be up to!

It was fully half an hour before Mr Armstrong joined

them in the living room, and he had a look of the cat that had finished the cream.

'I take it we're in your room,' he said to Jim, as he sat down beside him on the couch.

The boy said that he didn't mind at all.

'Well, thats good of you,' smiled the missionary. 'And I have a little thank-you present for you.'

He took a very small brown envelope from his inside pocket, and handed it to Jim.

For a minute the lad was embarrassed. He couldn't be offering him money, could he? But a glance at the old man's face reassured him that it wasn't anything as awkward as that.

'Wow!' gasped Jim, as he slid the contents of the envelope out on to his hand.

'How did you know ....?'

The two of them were so absorbed in each other that Mrs Armstrong thought she'd better explain what was going on.

'My husband is a stamp collector,' she told Mum Elliot. 'He keeps all his duplicates, and when we visit where there are young folk in the house, he gives them stamps as little presents. But ....'

Mum wondered what the but was going to be.

'But when he saw Jim's model sailing ships and aeroplanes, then caught sight of his stamp collection, he went through all the stamps he's brought with him to find ones with sailing ships and planes on them.'

'Now, that's what I call thoughtful,' said Mum Elliot.

'And I'm sure he'll do the same for Bob, Fred and Jane when he knows what their hobbies are.'

Jane smiled broadly, and tried to make up her mind which of her hobbies she would like to see on postage stamps.

Meanwhile, Mr Armstrong and Jim were in their own little world. The stamps were on a tray between them and they were going through them one by one, holding them carefully with tweezers.

'That's the Last Voyage of the Training-ship President Sarmieto,' Jim said. 'I've seen it in a stamp catalogue.'

'Quite right,' the missionary agreed. 'It's Argentinean, 1938...'

'What's that one?' the boy asked. 'It's from Afghanistan.'

'That's an aeroplane over Kabul from 1939. There are green and blue ones in the set as well as this orange one.'

Jim picked up another stamp.

'I've got this 1940 one of the Bulgarian mail plane. Bob gave it to me for my birthday.'

'What about these two?' asked the missionary. 'Do you have them?'

Jim looked at the two 1931 Cuban stamps. One showed a Fokker F10 flying over a beach, the other a Ford Trimotor flying over a forest.'

He shook his head. 'No,' he said. 'But they're great stamps!'

'And this one is a little bit special, and rather amusing too,' commented Mr Armstrong, picking up a stamp from Honduras. 'It's called The Flag of the Race. And it was produced in 1933 to mark the 441st anniversary of the departure of Columbus from Palos. There are six in the set.'

'The 441st?' said Jim

Mr Armstrong laughed aloud. 'That was exactly my

response. I too wondered why they'd not done them a year earlier!'

Jim looked at his companion and grinned.

'I've kept the best one till last,' the missionary said. 'Look at this.'

It was a New Zealand stamp, 1939, and it showed Captain Cook on the right, a chart of New Zealand in the middle, and the sailing ship Endeavour on the left.

'It's from a set of 13 all about the history of New Zealand. There's one showing the arrival of the Maoris in 1350, one of Abel Tasman with his ship and chart, one of HMS Britomart at Akaroa …'

'And you can keep the other nine till we come home or there will be no missionary meeting this evening,' his wife laughed.

Mr Armstrong jumped to his feet remarkably quickly for a man his age.

'I'm so sorry, Clara,' he said to Mum Elliot. 'When I get together with a stamp man over some interesting postage stamps, I just don't notice the passage of time.'

'You can say that again,' laughed his wife. 'And again … and again … and again!'

Jim liked the expression 'stamp man' and hung on to it for future use.

'You coming to the meeting, young man?' his friend asked.

'We're all going,' Jim told him. 'We always do.'

'I like to see the young in church,' Mrs Armstrong said, as they left the house.

Mum Elliot agreed. 'We've taken them since they were six weeks old,' she said. 'We want them to be as much at home in the house of God as in their very own home.'

'Pa Armstrong and I have spent years working as missionaries,' their visitor said. 'But you're being missionaries here right in your own home with your fine family.'

The young Elliots listened as Mr Armstrong spoke about the work he and his wife did in Central America. They heard about people becoming Christians, and others who had shown an interest for a while then decided that Christianity wasn't for them. When the old missionary spoke about those who had gone to church then left, his face creased until it looked as though he was going to cry.

'Let's pray,' he said suddenly.

Everyone bowed their heads and closed their eyes. There was silence for a minute or two before Mr Armstrong led them in prayer for the young people who had turned their backs on Jesus. And Jim knew, he knew for sure, that the silence was because his old friend was weeping.

Back home after the meeting there was plenty to talk about. The whole family wanted to know more about the work the Armstrongs did, each from their own point of view. Dad Elliot wanted to know what the people were able to grow in such a remote area. His wife asked about the children, and about health care. Fred was interested in how the missionaries travelled between villages in the jungle. How the Armstrongs had set about learning the language intrigued Bob. Young Jane wanted to know what the village children learned in the little mission school that Mrs Armstrong ran. And Jim listened to it all, as he had listened to so many other discussions during missionaries' visits, and deep inside him something stirred. He loved the Lord Jesus, and he did tell his friends about him. Did that make him a missionary? the boy wondered. Do you have to go to a foreign country to be a missionary?

Supper time the following night was a hilarious affair. Mr Armstrong had discovered that the Elliot family was originally from Scotland, just north of the border between Scotland and England. Their ancestors had left Scotland for Canada in the middle of the 19th Century.

'Would you believe it?' he asked. 'That's just where the Armstrongs come from too.'

'You'll never stop him now!' laughed the missionary's wife. 'When it comes to talking about Scotland, my dear man can talk for every single clan!'

'Did you know that the Scots borderers were experts in raiding over the border into England?' Mr Armstrong asked. 'They brought sheep and cattle back with them, and anything else they could find. They were called the Border Rievers.'

Mr Elliot, who knew a thing or two himself, pointed out that the English were also clever border rievers, and that both the Elliots and the Armstrongs had probably lost cattle and sheep to them too.'

Jane's mind, which was clouded by sleepiness, thought of the sheep on the Scottish border hills. Imagine if one were separated from the others during a raid. It wouldn't know whether to follow the flock that was being taken away or to try to get home again. It would be scared and lost. A shiver went through the child as she thought what that might feel like.

'What's in your mind?' Mrs Armstrong asked. She had her arm around Jane's shoulder and had felt her shiver.

Jane explained what she'd been thinking about to the comfortable lady at her side. She didn't even realise that everyone else was silent and listening.

Mrs Armstrong listened to Jane's fears for the lost sheep, and then very quietly she started to sing. The Elliots all knew the song she was singing, and before their visitor reached the end of the first verse, they had all joined in. Strangely though, despite eight people singing together, they sang so quietly it was as though the song was just a whisper in the silence of the evening. Jane, who knew that the song was based on a story Jesus told, saw her father pick up his Bible for family worship, and she guessed correctly the verses he would read.

'Jesus told them this parable. "Suppose one of you has a hundred sheep and loses one of them. Does he not leave the ninety-nine in the open country and go after the lost sheep until he finds it. And when he finds it, he joyfully puts it on his shoulders and goes home. Then he calls his friends and neighbours together and says, 'Rejoice with me: I have found my lost sheep.'"'

Jim had trouble getting to sleep that night, partly because he was in a put-up bed that wasn't as comfortable as his own one, and partly because his mind kept going back to the young people Mr Armstrong had told them about, the ones who had seemed interested in becoming Christians but who then stopped going to church. He pictured the old missionary's face as he spoke about them, and saw his sad and solemn expression. The boy knew it was a very solemn thing not to believe in Jesus; it was the most serious and solemn of all things.

He turned over and tried sleeping on his other side. And it was as though his mind turned over at the same time. With a sense of relief Jim remembered that his father and mother, his brothers and sister all trusted in the Lord Jesus, and all believed his promise that one day they would be with him in heaven. Somehow that made it easier to fall asleep, because that's exactly what Jim did.

Onwards and Upwards

Taking one last look around his old classroom in 1941, so many memories tumbled into Jim's mind and most of them made him smile. 'I don't suppose my teachers in Benson Polytechnic High School will wallpaper the classroom with my artwork,' he thought. 'I've been a big fish in a little pond till now, and I'm going to have to learn to be a little fish in a big pond.' For the last time he walked out of the school into the yard and across to the bicycle rack. As he removed his bike from the rack, another memory made him laugh aloud. His schoolmate, Dick, who was playground monitor for a year, used to tease him because he was forever running late. Jim remembered many mornings when he'd heard the school bell ringing as he cycled down 80th Street. He could almost feel the crunch on the gravel outside the Gable Funeral Home as he did a racing turn though the church grounds next door before skidding to a halt in a cloud of dust right beside the bicycle rack, just as Dick was about to give up on him being on time. 'Guess I'm going to have to grow up,' he thought. 'But that's quite exciting.'

Dad Elliot also had growing up on his mind, and he reckoned it was time to have a serious talk with his third son.

'When your brothers were 14, I told them what I'm going to tell you,' he said to Jim, 'and I want you to listen real hard. Your mother and I have tried to bring you up in the Christian way. When you've done wrong, you've been punished for it. Though I hope we've always let a subject drop as soon as the punishment was over.'

'I'm grateful for that,' Jim told his dad, 'and also that if I did something really wrong you always waited until we were alone before you punished me.'

Mr Elliot thought for a moment. 'That's because you deserved punishment not humiliation,' he explained. 'But you're 14 now, and I reckon that's past the age when a father should spank his son. When you were a boy you put your trust in the Lord Jesus as your Saviour. You're a young man now, and you are responsible to the Lord for your actions, not to me. But remember this, there will have been times in the past when you got off with doing something wrong because your mother and I didn't know anything about it, but God knows everything, and he has his own way of punishing.'

What his father said to him that day stayed in Jim's mind for the rest of his life, which was exactly what Dad Elliot intended.

However, life with his father was not always a serious affair, and one thing Jim especially liked was when the family went to stock shows. He enjoyed walking around listening to the farmers talking amongst themselves. At a visit to a stock show in 1941, Jim wandered among the men hearing much the same as he'd heard before in previous years.

'Fine bull that,' one man said to another, as they stood beside an American Brown Swiss bull.

'Nothing like the old breeds,' his neighbour replied. 'That one started off with 130 head of Braunvieh imported to the States from Switzerland in the 1870s and 80s; and it's come a long way since then. Is that what you breed?'

'No, I've a Charolais bull,' the first man said. 'And I'm working towards a Charolais herd. It took a bit of getting used to a solid white beast when they first came in about seven years ago, but I think they have a future.'

Jim could remember when he'd first seen a Charolais cow, and he'd thought it looked odd.

As he wandered round the show, a snippet of information caught Jim's ear.

'British White cattle,' he heard someone say.

'What are they?' wondered Jim. 'Charolais are French.'

He stood beside the little group of farmers who were talking together and listened to what was being said.

'The British Government ordered a shipment of British White Cattle to be brought over to America,' a tall dark man said.

'Why did they do that?' someone asked.

'It's to safeguard the breed in case of a German invasion,' explained the tall man. 'The breed is to be kept pure here in the US. There's to be no interbreeding. Then, if there is an invasion and the breed is endangered, the UK can be restocked from here eventually.'

The speaker saw Jim's interest in the subject. 'The cattle that were shipped here come from the oldest British White Cattle herd that was established over 200 years ago. That's too precious a heritage to risk losing.'

Jim agreed, and his dad was really interested when he heard all about it.

'You could be a farmer,' Dad Elliot said. 'But you're one of these fortunate and unfortunate boys who are good at a whole number of things.'

'Why fortunate and unfortunate?' Jane asked, thinking that was a very strange thing to say.

'Well, if a boy is good at just one thing, then it's clear what he should do with his life,' her father explained. 'But your brother is good at so many things that he'll have trouble choosing between them.'

That made sense to Jane, but Jim was quite happy to major in architectural drawing in Benson, and he certainly was good at it.

'Did you understand that complicated elevation?' his friend, Dick, asked him one day.

'Yes,' said Jim. 'It's not complicated if you think about it.'

Jim took out his notebook, balanced on his left leg, and rested his notebook on his right knee.

'You look like an ostrich!' Dick laughed.

Ostrich or not, within a few short sentences and quick sketches Jim had explained to his friend what he had not understood in class.

'You should be a teacher,' said Dick. 'I'd get better marks if you were.'

Jim Elliot grinned. 'That's the second careers guidance I've had today. This morning one of the teachers was trying to persuade me that my future was on the stage! I don't mind taking part in school plays, but can you imagine how boring it would be to have to act the same part twice a day for a month. My brain would rot!'

'No it wouldn't,' Dick screwed up his face. 'But you'd forget where you were and end up preaching to the audience!'

Jim's mind wasn't always on preaching, especially when there was a football around, though his style was thought to be a little unusual.

'You look like a big knock-kneed moose in your football gear,' Dick told him often. 'And you play like one too.'

But there was more to football than just playing it. And in Jim's second year in High School the National Football League was a source of great interest.

'It's not fair,' DK announced, in the schoolyard one day. 'The Chicago Bears were set to win the NFL, but some of the best players are away to the war.'

'It's the same for every team,' his pal reminded him.

'No, it's not,' argued DK. 'I read in yesterday's paper that Halas has left the Bears to join the Navy! He's one of their best players.'

'The Washington Redskins won at the Griffith Stadium last Saturday, and some of their best players are in the Armed Forces too,' Jim said.

'Here we go!' laughed DK. 'You're just sticking up for the Redskins because you're second generation from a Washington homestead. There's no way the Redskins will win the NFL! The Chicago Bears won it last year and the year before. And they'll be champions again this year even with Halas in the Navy!'

'You wait and see,' Jim laughed. 'If enough of the Redskins are called into the Armed Forces they'll ask me to join the team!'

Dick, who had joined them by then, roared with laughter. 'The Washington Redskins used to be called the Boston Braves. And they'd have to be brave to ask you to join the team!'

As the months passed, the tension over the National Football League rose to fever pitch. And when the semi-final results came out, both Jim and DK had good reason to be pleased.

'I told you the Redskins would win!' Jim teased his friend.

'Well they haven't yet,' DK reminded him. 'The final's not till 13th December. I'd do anything to get to Washington to see the Redskins beaten by the Chicago Bears.'

Jim laughed. 'Don't waste your fare on a ticket, because that's just not going to happen.'

'So they've picked you for the team after all!' DK teased. 'I guess that's it settled.'

Their excitement grew as the day of the match approached, and a knife could have cut the tension on match day. It took all of Jim's Christian faith not to tease DK quite mercilessly on 14th December, because the Chicago Bears didn't stand a chance. The final score, 14-6 to the Washington Redskins, told the whole story.

Although Jim was just a teenager, he normally carried a little Bible on top of his pile of school books. He was not in the least embarrassed or ashamed of it. Not only that, but he was always ready to speak about his faith. If there was a little huddle of Benson students standing together, Jim was quite likely to be found in the middle of it explaining something from the Bible.

'I hear there's a boy who fancies himself as a preacher,' a new girl said, one day in school. 'Bit of a wimp, is he?'

'See for yourself,' her friend replied. 'That's him coming along the corridor at 50 miles an hour!'

'Guess I got it wrong,' admitted the newcomer. 'He's one good-looking guy! I'd pictured a pale scrawny boy, not someone as well built and good-looking as him. His tan goes well with his gorgeous brown hair too.'

'Are you interested in Christianity?' asked her companion.

'Not till now,' the girl laughed. 'But I can feel an interest developing as we speak!'

As Jim went through High School, he took every opportunity he could to speak at meetings. To start with he needed to try out his talks before giving them. That's where Dick came in.

'Do you have time to listen for quarter of an hour?' Jim asked his friend.

'Depends what I'd be listening to.'

'Good Bible stuff.'

'OK. But a quarter of an hour's the limit. If you don't strike oil in quarter of an hour you can stop boring!'

The first few times Dick listened to his talks, he just burst out laughing. And that didn't best please Jim. However, before long the teenaged preacher developed a style that made it hard to laugh. And when his subject was hell, as it was from time to time, that was no laughing matter at all.

'You wouldn't think the war in Europe would have so much effect on us here in the US,' Dick commented one day, as he and his friend were waiting for the bus home.

'Just think how much more difficult it must be in England. At least we have buses, even if there are fewer than they used to be. I heard that in England transport is a real problem.'

'I read somewhere that in the blackout, buses and cars have to travel with no lights on. They must creep along the streets and be a real danger to pedestrians.'

'There's not even the sight of a bus creeping here today,' Dick announced. 'I think we should try to hitch a lift home.'

That was the start of the two boys hitching home from

school, and they continued to do it whether or not a bus was coming. Not only did it save them a nickel a day, but it allowed them to spend more time together, and that meant more talking.

'If you could do anything in the world, what would it be?' Dick asked one day, as they waited at the roadside to hitch a lift.

Jim grinned. 'I'd be President of the United States of America. Just think how much influence you could have. And an out-and-out Christian President could make a real difference to the country. What about you?'

Dick smiled. 'That would depend on you,' he said. 'I take it you would appoint me to some high office in the White House!'

'Would you like to come back to my house tomorrow?' Jim asked his friend. 'It's not the White House yet, but it's home.'

'Sure thing,' said Dick. 'Look forward to that.'

After school the following day the two boys hitched a lift to quite near the Elliot home, then walked the rest.

'The kettle's on,' Mum said, with a welcoming smile. 'And the flapjacks will be ready as soon as you are.'

As they ate their way through some flapjacks, almost burning their tongues in the process, Jim set about organising his friend in order to give them time to relax together.

'Do you like goats?' he asked.

Dick screwed up his face. He knew goats could be a bit unpredictable.

'OK,' laughed Jim. 'I'll feed the goats and stoke the furnace. You feed the chickens and rabbits. Then we can talk while I tidy the yard.'

'That's fine by me,' Dick agreed, thinking that his friend had quite a lot to do outside of school, though he didn't seem to mind it one bit.

'There are a couple of errands to run,' Jim said, when they'd finished the yard. 'We can talk on the way if you come with me.'

Dick nodded. 'There's no point in wasting time when we've a world to sort out.'

And the pair of them set off on Mum Elliot's errands, talking all the way. Jim's conversations moved easily from subject to subject – from football to prayer, from rearing rabbits to Christ rising from the dead, from tobogganing on Mt Hood to the miracles Jesus performed. Dick often thought how much part of his life Jim's faith was. It certainly wasn't only for Sundays.

'Mum's expecting you to stay for supper,' Jim said, on the way back. 'Is that OK with your folks?'

'They'll expect me when they see me,' Dick grinned. 'My mother's heard about your mother's cooking!'

As the family sat round the table for supper, everyone fell silent for Dad Elliot to thank the Lord for their food.

'It doesn't take courage to say grace before eating a meal here,' thought Dick. 'But Jim does it at school too. And I reckon that takes real courage.'

A Near Miss

Jim Elliot and Dick Fisher were accompanied by another friend, Werner Durtschi, on some hair-raising adventures. At least one of them might have cost Jim's life.

'You'd really love to come camping,' Jim told his two friends, for about the tenth time that day.

Dick looked at the grey sky and wondered if this was really true.

Taking silence as a definite yes, Jim rattled out his ideas without stopping long enough for either of the other two to say no.

'We could go to the second-hand shops to buy anything we need.'

'Trust him to think of that,' Dick grinned. 'Being broke would have been my first objection.'

'Then on Friday right after school we could hitch a ride and see how far we get.'

'What about food?' asked Dutch (as Werner was always called).

'We've got guns, haven't we?' Jim said, as though roast chicken, bread rolls and milk could be shot everywhere in Oregon.

It didn't really take much persuading to get his friends to agree, especially as they'd enjoyed some camping trips together in the past. As always, they prayed for God's blessing on the trip before they went. Years later, Dick wrote, 'I often thought if we had a guardian angel, he was kept on his toes and didn't get much sleep either.'

'OK, you guys,' said Jim, in the organising voice for which he was well known, 'while one of us stands by the road to flag down a driver, the other two should duck behind the hedge. I can't see anyone stopping for us otherwise.'

The boys looked at each other and laughed their agreement. There they were, three teenagers, each of them with a rucksack and a rifle, and each rifle with a tin can over its barrel to keep out the rain.

Taking turns at being the flagger-down, they eventually made their way out of town and into the Oregon countryside. Perhaps they were more grateful for the ride than one family they travelled with was for their company. When the driver slowed down to pick up what he thought was one hitchhiker, he assumed he had plenty of room in his car. So he had. But when another two lads emerged with all their camping gear it took a bit of pushing to get them all into the car!

The following day, three stomachs were rumbling with hunger when the boys passed a lake and heard a duck quacking.

'Shoosh!' said Jim. He was such a quick thinker that he always seemed to be the one giving orders. 'I heard a duck.' Pushing a shell into the breech of his rifle, he aimed ... and nothing happened. His rifle had jammed. Half a minute later, Dutch shot from behind Jim's back. But he missed the duck by a whisker. By then Dick's rifle was loaded, and he was determined not to miss his dinner. Hitting the duck fair and square, it plummeted into the lake. Which was exactly what the three boys felt like doing a few minutes later, when a woman came running in their direction shouting something about a tame duck, and about them being murderers. They had assumed that a duck with unclipped wings was wild, and certainly not a pet. Jim fished the main ingredient for their supper out of the lake before racing after his friends. Although they felt bad about it, the duck was very dead so there was no point in not having it roasted. They did pray for God to comfort the woman if it really was her tame duck.

Not long afterwards they were off on another camping weekend, this time on the banks of the Columbia River.

'This is an amazing river,' Dick said. 'Where it cuts through rock gorges the roar of the water is deafening.'

'It's the only waterway to cross the Cascade Mountains,' Jim told his friends. He was always a rich source of information, some of it interesting but pretty useless. 'It drains a huge inland area along the border between Washington and Oregon.'

'When the Snake River and the Willamette join it just inland of Portland it makes for a mighty flow into the sea at Astoria,' Dutch added. 'But the Latourell Falls are my favourite part of the river, especially right behind the falls where you get the full effect of the water.'

The boys hiked on to the Latourell Falls.

'Let's go to the top first,' Dick suggested. 'It's a strange feeling when you look over the edge.'

Scrambling up the 249 feet to the top of the falls was no problem for the three of them. They were well used to physical exercise.

'Take it slowly,' said Dutch, as they eased their way to the edge of the falls. Holding hands in case one of them should become dizzy, they looked over the top.

'It's the most terrific thing I've ever seen,' Jim shouted, above the roar of the water. 'It's just like looking down from a cloud.'

The air around them was thick with moisture. The roar below them felt as though it made the ground shake. And the spray the falls sent up seemed to come to meet them as they looked over the edge. It was an awe-inspiring moment.

Having had the excitement of the top of the falls, they clambered down to the pool at the bottom, then went along the narrow path that led right behind the waterfall. Damp rock behind them, and a raging torrent of water cascading down in front of them, silenced the boys for a minute or two. The magnificence of it made them hold their breath almost as if by breathing out they would spoil the whole effect.

'If this is what God does on earth,' Jim said, above the water's roar, 'just imagine what eternity will be like!'

It was on another camping trip with his friends that Jim nearly found out what eternity was like. Dick, who had just shot a buzzard, was climbing over a barbed wire fence to retrieve the bird, when he accidentally discharged his rifle. The shot went through Jim's hair! In the stunned silence that followed the gun's report, the boys sank to the ground in sheer relief.

'Are you all right?' Dick breathed.

'Yea,' said Jim, more than a little shakily. 'Yea, I'm OK.'

Dick was shivering. 'That was a close thing.'

Jim rubbed his head thankfully. 'The brain's still intact,' he said, trying to take the tension out of the situation.

'Thank God for that,' Dick breathed, and that was probably his most heartfelt prayer ever.

There was some serious talking done that day about God being sovereign and in control of all things, and about how everyone is dependent on the Lord for the very next breath they take.

Not all Saturdays were spent on camping trips. In fact, Jim and Dick spent most Saturdays working with Bert Elliot, who had set up a little business for himself. Having bought a truck, he earned some income by collecting rubbish, recycling what he could and dumping the rest.

'Up you go!' Bert told the boys, when his truck was ready to roll.

The pair of them had several jobs to do. First, they had to help load the rubbish on to the truck at every pick-up point. Then they had to fend off seagulls that saw it as their Saturday entertainment to duck and dive all around them, trying to find something tasty to eat among the garbage.

'They're fierce creatures,' Dick yelled, above the sound of the truck's engine.

Grabbing an old strip-lighting tube, he brandished it in the air to keep the birds at bay. Jim found another one and did the same. They must have looked a pretty pair as the truck sped from stop to stop with them appearing to do some kind of war dance with strip lights waving in the air and excited seagulls for company! Rather than disposing of the tubes when they reached the dump, they kept them as weapons for the following Saturday.

'Right you guys,' Bert said, when the truck was ready for emptying. 'Take out what can be recycled and ditch the rest.'

Jim's job was to remove the glass bottles, and Dick looked for bricks that were still in fairly good shape. It was left to Bert to look for other things. And over the months he discovered that people threw out some very interesting things. There was a bearskin rug – complete with head.

'I'll find a home for that,' he said. 'Imagine throwing this fine fellow out!'

Then there was a bed that could be sold, and chairs that were still useable. Stoves were dumped fairly often, and if they were not good enough to sell as they stood, they were kept for spare parts.

'What that?' Bert asked himself, opening a box.

'It looks like a dentist's equipment,' suggested Dick.

In fact, it turned out to be a set of autopsy tools – medical instruments used by a pathologist to do post mortem examinations.

'Can I have them?' Jim asked.

His older brother grinned. 'Suppose so,' he said. 'I can't imagine any doctor is going to buy his next set of instruments off a garbage truck!'

The instruments inspired Jim to take a class in taxidermy. And the first creature he stuffed was a seagull caught one Saturday from on top of the rubbish truck.

Looking like vagabonds after sifting through the rubbish at the dump, Jim and Dick gathered up the day's takings of glass bottles and headed to a shop to redeem the money on them.

'Not them again,' sighed the girl behind the counter, to her colleague who had just started that day. 'They come here twice every Saturday … and ….. look at the mess of them!'

Her friend thought the two young men looked like tramps!

'Give them the money, or whatever they want to buy with it, and get them out the shop. They'll give the place a bad name.'

The boys were not unaware of the effect they had on the shop assistants, and it amused them greatly. Mind you, they were no doubt careful who didn't see them dressed for their Saturday job on the garbage truck!

'We fairly put the girls off us,' Dick commented, as they left the shop one day.

'And long may it continue like that,' agreed Jim.

His friend turned and gave him a long hard look.

'Well,' Jim said, 'it's like this. We're young and free and can choose what we do. If we had serious girlfriends we'd not be able to head off on camping weekends. We'd always have to consult them about what we wanted to do. We've a lot of living to do before we get serious about girls.'

Dick grinned, and thought about the many times he'd been beginning to get friendly with a girl at some occasion or other, when his friend sidled up to him and said quietly in the passing, 'Beware, Fisher, beware.'

It wasn't that Jim didn't appreciate a good-looking girl when he saw one; it was just that he felt he had other things he had to consider. And as his friends began to pair off as they went through High School, he really did have to think the issue through. For one thing, Jim didn't have as much free time as his friends, as he had a lot of work to do at home. Also when Dad Elliot and Bert were away preaching sometimes at weekends, Jim felt responsible for things at home and didn't go out with his friends and their girls.

'But there's more to it than that,' he explained to Dick, as they walked along the road one day. 'My priority is to serve the Lord. And it may be that having a wife and children would limit what I could do for him.'

'What do you mean?'

Jim thought for a moment or two.

'Well, supposing the Lord wants me to be a missionary in a place where it might not be safe to take a woman, or somewhere the climate wasn't suitable for small children,' the teenager suggested. 'I'd have to seriously consider whether, in fact, he wanted me to be married at all.'

Mission work was never far from Jim's mind, as Dutch discovered one day when he found his friend doing track training.

'Planning on entering a race?' asked Dutch.

Jim shook his head and explained that he was trying to harden his body to cope with the tough missionary life.

In April 12th, 1945, news spread like wildfire that President Franklin D Roosevelt had died suddenly and unexpectedly. America was plunged into mourning. The Second World War was still raging, and America was deeply involved in it. Suddenly, throughout the United States, there was a feeling of uncertainty, of confusion, even of fear. Harry S Truman immediately succeeded President Roosevelt in the White House, and the nation took a deep breath as it waited to see what would happen next.

'We're going to hold a special assembly this afternoon,' Jim was told at school. 'And we want you to speak at it.'

Although he was known as a fine speaker, and although he had taken part in services, debates and discussions, this was a whole new ballgame for Jim Elliot. He had just a few hours to prepare a speech to pay tribute to the late President in front of the entire student body and staff of Benson Polytechnic High School. Excused from lessons for the morning, Jim headed for the current affairs books to discover what he could about Roosevelt, and to his Bible to know what best to say.

Relying on God to help him, Jim stood up that afternoon and paid tribute to Franklin Delano Roosevelt. He outlined the man's life, from his childhood in Hyde Park, New York, through his legal career to his election to the State Senate when he was still in his twenties. But, Jim said, it would be his wartime presidency for which he would be remembered.

'In August 1941, President Roosevelt met with Prime Minister Winston Churchill at sea, and they drafted the Atlantic Charter, aligning the United States with Britain. Less than three months later, he did all he could to try to maintain peace with Japan by addressing a personal message of peace to Emperor Hirohito.'

Jim's audience listened attentively, remembering back to the hope that day had given them.

'But the following day, December 7th 1941, the Japanese attacked Pearl Harbour and so plunged our country into war. Although voices were raised against President Roosevelt, the election last year, returning him to power, was a measure of the esteem in which he was held.'

'That was one of the finest speeches I've ever heard,' one teacher commented to a colleague.

There was no response. The other man was too emotional to reply.

There was a strange irony in Jim Elliot being asked to deliver that tribute, because his Christian conviction was that he should not be involved in politics at all. Most Christians would not agree with him. Jim's lack of political involvement, however, did not prevent him from presenting a memorable tribute to the man who had steered the United States through most of the Second World War, a man who had spoken out for human freedom and who had laboured to establish lasting peace through the United Nations.

Off to College!

'Two more days till you leave for Wheaton College,' Jane said, to her older brother. 'It's going to be strange here without you. Why did you choose to go so far away?'

'I'm sure that's where God wants me to study,' Jim replied. 'And it is still in America.'

Jane looked at her atlas. 'But it's not exactly round the corner,' she smiled. 'There's a whole lot of America between here and Wheaton.'

She traced over the page of her map with her finger. 'It's right through Oregon, Idaho, Wyoming, Nebraska and Iowa before you reach Illinois.'

Then she grinned. 'I know what it is. You can't bear to be too far from the sea. Having chosen to leave Portland, you're heading for Lake Michigan.'

Jim laughed. 'Now, there was me thinking that your geography was good because you knew all the states between here and Wheaton. But it's not, or you'd know that Lake Michigan isn't a sea!'

'But it's big enough to be a sea,' she said.

'I don't suppose I'll see much of Lake Michigan anyway,' Jim said. 'It's right on the other side of Chicago from Wheaton, and Chicago's a big city.'

Suddenly Jane became serious.

'How are you going to pay your fees at Wheaton, and what are you going to live on?'

Jim shrugged his shoulders.

'I don't actually know the answer to these questions, but I know God. And if he wants me to study at Wheaton, he'll provide everything I need there.'

Two months after arriving, Jim was able to write home to say that God had indeed given him everything he needed. A friend gave him a gift of money, he won a scholarship and found a part-time job.'

'All I need has been supplied by God's ever-tender loving-kindness,' he wrote to his parents, back home in Portland.

Even though God had provided Jim with enough money, the young student was very careful how he spent it.

'I'll have chicken with salad and fresh fruit,' he told the girl behind the college meal counter.

'You don't eat much,' a boy in front of him commented.

Jim looked at his fellow student's plate of pastry pie and beans.

'Maybe not,' Jim agreed. 'But I eat what's good for me.'

'Are you in training?' the other student asked.

'Yea,' agreed Jim. 'I'm in training.'

'Football?'

'No, I've taken up wrestling,' Jim admitted. 'But I'm in training for serving God rather than for wrestling. That's much more important.'

Jim had never wrestled before going to Wheaton, but he made it into the university team in his first year! He had just the right build for the job, and thanks to his diet being high in fresh fruit and vegetables there was no flab covering his muscles. Jim was very firm in his conviction that wrestling was a sport, not an outlet for aggression, though he had problems convincing his mother! In answer to a letter she sent warning him how dangerous wrestling was, he wrote to her describing his first injury, which he didn't think was serious at all.

'My first evil effect from this 'ungodly' thing, as Granny (an old friend in Wheaton) calls wrestling, showed up on Saturday. It is a puffing of the inner flanges of the ear, commonly called a 'cauliflower ear.' It's not serious, though Granny thought it was terrible for me to be singing hymns on my way to the wrestling match! She could hardly believe it when I told her that we prayed before fights!'

When Jim wrestled, he wrestled hard. John, his opponent one Saturday afternoon, discovered that. If he thought that a bout with a Christian would be easy, he had some serious re-thinking to do. That evening Jim described the match to his friends.

'John decided to go for it right away; there was no pussy-footing around for him. Before I knew where I was, he'd grabbed my ankles with his arms and had my back to the mat in an ankle lace. He must have thought I was covered in butter, because I bridged my back and was out of it on to my stomach while he still thought he had me.'

'What happened then?' a friend asked, while Jim took a drink of water. He was still thirsty after his afternoon's exertion.

Jim laughed. 'I locked my arms round John's body and took him to the mat. He squirmed out of that, and I used an arm bar to turn him over for a pin.'

'Well done!' laughed his friends.

'It was my turn to end on the mat then, when John caught me cross-face, swung me round and had me down. But I was on my feet before he'd had time to think what to do next. He left himself open after that, and I ducked my head under his arm, came up behind him, and did a lift that put him on the mat and completed the takedown.'

'No wonder they call you the India Rubber Man!' one of his friends laughed. 'You can tie yourself in knots in the ring, and untie yourself and escape like Harry Houdini.'

'Well I didn't learn my escapes from Houdini,' Jim laughed. 'He died the year before I was born!'

'I'd love to have seen him,' a student said, 'especially doing one of his escapes from a locked trunk under water.'

Jim shook his head. 'That's not for me. I'll stick to escaping from body locks, ankle laces and cradles. At least they're done on dry land!'

Although he enjoyed wrestling, Jim saw it as a way of keeping himself fit in order to serve God. He prepared himself in other ways too. For example, Jim set his alarm to waken him early enough each morning that he had time to read his Bible and pray before beginning classes. And that must have been quite early, as some classes began as early as 7.30 am!

Jim Elliot was not only concerned about his own growth as a Christian, he was also interested in his sister, Jane.

'Begin each day with private reading of God's Word and prayer,' he wrote to her. 'John Bunyan said that "Sin will keep you from this Book (the Bible), or this Book will keep you from sin." From the very first, as you begin high school, give out gospel tracts to those you meet. Make a bold start – it's easier that way, rather than trying to begin halfway through. Memorize Bible verses as you travel on the street car.'

Jim finished that letter by saying that he wished

someone had given him that advice when he went to high school. He was talking from personal experience.

'Are you going home for the summer?' a friend asked, as the session at Wheaton drew to a close.

'I certainly am,' said Jim. 'And I'm looking forward to it.'

'How are you getting there?'

Jim took a handful of coins from his trouser pocket.

'I don't think I'll be flying on this lot!' he laughed. 'So I guess it will be hitch-hiking for me.'

'From here to Portland!' gasped his friend. 'You'll be lucky if you get home on time to come back next term.'

Later Jim described part of that journey in a letter to his brother. 'On Monday night I was walking a hard stretch of pavement at Cedar Rapids, Iowa, when a new Studebaker pick-up lived up to its name. "Where are you going?" I queried. "California," replied a tough marine sergeant. And I climbed in, thinking of God's word to Moses, "My presence shall go with you, and I will give you rest." We slept for three hours on Tuesday morning in the truck, then pushed on through Nebraska, and a good bit of Wyoming by midnight.'

'At Casper, Wyoming, the marine's ex-father-in-law owns a tavern. I slept in my clothes on a smelly couch in the back room and had two eggs and black coffee for breakfast when I woke up. Mid afternoon, I hitched on a coal-truck that took me to Cokeville. The Lord is good! After that an ancient Buick stopped, and a sailor gave me a lift. Unfortunately the Buick wasn't up to much and we had to stop often for fuel, water and oil. I drove for a while as the sailor slept. And while I was driving along there was a grinding crack in the engine … and we ground to a halt. That was a good excuse for a sleep and we both needed it. At 6 am a breakdown truck hitched us up and towed us to Boise. So your brother hitched a lift in a Buick that hitched a lift on a breakdown truck!'

'At Boise the sailor stayed with his car and I headed for the highway again and soon had another lift. I eventually arrived back home in Portland at lunchtime. The journey took 70 hours in 20 different vehicles and I beat the slow train home! And that's not all, because I still have my $1.32 in my pocket! Haven't we a wonderful Lord! I didn't wait any more than 15 minutes for a ride the whole journey. That was a real faith-strengthening experience!'

'What's Wheaton like?' Jane asked. 'I only know about the College because that's all you write home about.'

Jim wondered what his young sister would be interested in. 'Nearly 1000 acres of the land on that side of Chicago was claimed in the 1830s by two brothers, Jesse and Warren Wheaton. They were settlers from New England, and others followed soon after them. By 1880, there was a population of 1000. Now it's much bigger than that. I'll tell you one interesting bit of Wheaton's history. As the town grew, there was a ten-years long argument about whether Wheaton or Naperville should be the county town. Eventually a midnight raid on the Naperville courthouse settled it in 1867, when the county records were seized and taken back to Wheaton!'

'Was anyone from Wheaton College involved in the midnight raid?' Jane wanted to know.

'I'm afraid not, at least as far as I know,' smiled Jim. 'The College was just founded six years before that, in 1860,

66

though what became Wheaton College actually started as the Illinois Institute seven years before that. But I've not heard of any of the students being involved in midnight raids on courthouses. I think they would have been thrown out the College if they had!'

'Anything else interesting?' Jane asked.

'I suppose there is if you are interested in railroads. One of the earliest electric railroads was laid between Aurora, Elgin and Chicago in the 1890s. The corporation laid a 600-volt third rail system right from 52nd Avenue in Chicago all the way out to Aurora. Branch lines were built to Batavia and Elgin soon afterwards. The Aurora and Elgin line is nicknamed the 'Roarin' Elgin!' I'm not sure what kind of future it has though; I think one day most people will choose to travel by car.

Jane laughed at the thought.

'Ordinary people will never have cars,' said she. 'They'll always go by train.'

'I don't know about that,' Jim argued. 'I'm sure Rube Goldberg could invent one that ordinary people could afford.'

'Have you seen Rube Goldberg's invention for cracking an egg?' DK asked, when they met up.

Jim had not.

'I cut it out the paper months ago and kept it to show you,' his friend said. 'I'll go and get it.'

The pair of them had fun looking at the cartoon. Rube Goldberg was a very popular cartoonist at the time, and he specialised in drawing cartoons of complicated devices that were meant to do simple tasks. His complex plan for an egg-cracking machine was a very good example of that. After all, it only takes a knife or a spoon to crack an egg!

'What are you going to do all summer?' DK asked Jim, as they went for a stroll around Portland.

'I guess I'll do what I can to help Dad,' he replied. 'It's the busiest time of the year for him, and I'm sure he'll not say "no" to a hand with fruit-picking and the rest.'

DK laughed.

'I've a much better idea,' he said. 'You should study Rube Goldberg's designs then invent a machine that will pick fruit all by itself. Then when you are away from home your father can use the James Elliot Fruit-picker to help him do the work.

Dad Elliot shook his head when he heard DK's 'brilliant' suggestion.

'You can't enjoy a machine's company,' he told his son. 'And I'm looking forward to enjoying your company while you're at home.'

Jim and his father had many good talks over the course of that summer, but there was one thing that Jim just didn't seem to be able to make his father understand.

'Studying is a great opportunity,' the young man told his dad. 'But the problem is that it leaves so little time for what's really important.'

'Your studies are what's important, my boy,' Dad Elliot said. 'That's what you're at Wheaton for.'

'I know that,' agreed Jim. 'But I don't think you realise how many hours a day (and night) I sometimes have to work to keep up. And it leaves so little time for studying the Bible and praying and spending time with my Christian friends. Studying university subjects is important – and they are all good subjects – but I just wish I had more time to study the Bible.'

Dad Elliot, who for family reasons had never been a student beyond his school years, found all this hard to take in. It seemed to him that not having to work with your hands would leave you plenty of time to do everything you could possibly want to do.

That was a good summer for Jim Elliot. He enjoyed being out in all weathers and getting his hands dirty in the good Oregon soil. And he discovered how much he'd missed his friends. Dick, who had moved away from Portland, kept in touch by letters ... and by rather unusual letters. Not long after leaving home, Dick came across a book on the Chinook Indian language. He bought two copies, one for himself and one for Jim. For reasons best known to themselves, they wrote letters to each other in Chinook!

Summer in Mexico

'We'll meet at 3 o'clock prompt at the car,' the group of six decided. 'Now, do we all know what we're doing?'

'I'm going as song leader,' one student said. 'And the five of you are the speakers. And remember, you just have 10 minutes each. If any of you go over the time, the poor audience will stick to their seats! Imagine five speakers all speaking too long. We'd be there all night!'

Three o'clock found the six members of Wheaton's Student Foreign Missions Fellowship at the car and raring to go.

'When's the meeting?' Jim asked.

'7.45,' was the answer. 'But it will take us till then to get there and organised.'

The discussion in the car was all about missions, after all, that's what they were going to speak about to the university student group.

'Do you know that 18 women apply to become missionaries for every one man that applies?' one of his friends asked.

Jim shook his head. That figure, that he knew was accurate, horrified him. Why were men not willing to make mission their lives' work? It was something he just didn't understand.

That night, as they drove back to Wheaton, hunger pangs hit the young folk before they reached home.

'Let's stop for a snack,' one of the students suggested.

And all agreed that was just what they needed. The six of them strode into a café and placed their orders. As she brought out their food, the waitress was obviously interested in the carload of young people.

'Been out socialising?' she asked, curiously.

'No, not exactly socialising,' one lad replied. 'We've actually been at a university Christian group telling them about missions.'

The girl looked shocked. 'Are you lot missionaries?'

Jim explained that they were students themselves, but that they loved the Lord Jesus and wanted to share with everyone the good news that he is the one and only Saviour.'

'But this is America,' the girl laughed. 'You need to go to Africa to do that. America's a Christian country.'

It was late in the evening and the café wasn't busy. Which was just as well, because the waitress spent a long time speaking to her customers, and they tried their best to introduce her to Jesus. Eventually they had to leave the place, and they prayed for the young woman as soon as they slammed the car doors shut.

'America is just as much a mission field as Africa,' Jim commented. 'But that doesn't mean we should all stay here rather than going to other countries to preach the gospel.'

Jim Elliot had a notebook in which he kept things he really wanted to remember. One page, written while he was a student at Wheaton College, reads:

1700 languages have not a word of the Bible translated.

90% of people who volunteer to be missionaries never actually become missionaries.

64% of the world's population has never heard of Christ.

5,000 people in the world die every hour.

The population of India equals the combined populations of North America, Africa and South America. There is one missionary for every 71,000 people in India.

There is one Christian worker for every 50,000 people in foreign lands, while there is one to every 500 in the United States.

'Would you like to visit my folks with me?' Ron Harris, a fellow student, asked Jim in the spring of 1947.

'As you know, they are missionaries in Mexico. Six weeks with them would let you see what being a missionary is really like. That's something you can't learn in a college.'

Jim jumped at the chance. And in June, the two young men set off for Mexico – hitchhiking as usual. They didn't leave a record of how many lifts they needed to travel from Illinois, through Missouri, Oklahoma, Texas and eventually to Mexico itself.

One day another student travelling south joined the pair of them. His name was Ben.

'You'll have to watch yourself if you're going anywhere near San Juan,' a truck driver told them, as they drove through Missouri. 'The volcano there looks ready to blow the big one.'

Jim's eyes lit with interest.

'Do you know the story of the Parícutin?' the driver, a Mexican, asked.

73

Ben was about to answer that he did, but Jim got in first.

'We're not up-to-date on it, so tell us what you know.'

That suited the driver quite well. On a long drive there was nothing he liked better than talking about Mexico.

'The volcano was born on my 39th birthday, 20th February 1943, in a flat cornfield belonging to a man called Dionisio Pulido. There had been a vent in the field for years, but that day a small explosion took everyone by surprise, and that was followed by gusts of steam and sulphur fumes as well as volcanic ash. It was in the local papers at the time. If they'd guessed what was going to happen in the next four years it would have made the New York Times!'

'What did happen?' asked Jim.

'I was just going to tell you that,' the driver laughed. 'Your friend's are not as impatient as you are.'

Ben smiled to himself. As he knew the history of Parícutin he could afford to be patient with the driver spinning it out. In any case, they had a long journey ahead of them and plenty of time to spare.

'By midnight that night the volcanic cone was 20 feet high, and growing. By midnight the next night it was 100 feet high.'

'That's some growth,' Jim whistled.

The truck driver ignored him. 'And by the end of the week, it was over 550 feet high. That's when the name Parícutin Volcano stuck.'

'What kind of volcano is it?'

The driver didn't know, but Ben did.

'It's a cinder cone,' he explained. 'That's the simplest kind. They are built from particles and blobs of congealed lava blown out from a single vent. As the underground gas builds up and explodes the lava is blown violently into the air, where it breaks up into small fragments and solidifies. Then it falls as cinders around the vent and eventually forms a vaguely circular cone.'

'Well I never!' said the driver. 'I'll remember that.'

Jim turned to him and asked if he knew anything else about Parícutin.

'Sure do,' the man said, settling down to continue his story. 'And I wouldn't have wanted to be Dionisio Pulido for anything. Within weeks just about all his land was covered with ash. And only two things grow on volcanic ash – scientists coming to see what's going on and nosey tourists who can't keep away from a drama!'

'What's doing with it now?' Jim asked, when the driver had finish laughing at his own joke.

'Parícutin is over 1000 feet high now, and it's blowing its top good style. Not only that, but there are some new flows out of the base of the cone now too.'

'What causes that to happen?' queried Jim.

'Your clever friend will know that better than I do,' the driver laughed, handing the question over the Ben.

'It's just slumping and landsliding causing cracks where the base of the cone is unstable.'

'Told you he would know,' laughed the driver. 'Have you any other technical information I could quote to impress hitchhikers?'

Ben grinned, took a deep breath, and gave him the lot. 'The Parícutin Volcano belongs to the Trans-Mexican Volcanic belt, and to the monogenetic volcanic field of Michoacan-Guanajuato. The Michoacan-Guanajuato is mainly made up of cinder cones, which reach their maximum density in the Parícutin area. During its first phase, the Parícutin ejected pyroclastic materials, with volumes of over 6,000,000 cubic yards per day. Initially large-size clasts were dominant, but fine ash and lapilli gradually took over, and that's what's being blasted out now. This is called it's cinder phase.'

The driver fumbled with his lumber-jacket pocket and took out a sheet of paper and a well-chewed pencil.

'Can I have that in writing?' he roared with laughter. 'And I'll try to learn it off by heart! A few more hitchhikers like you and I'll be offered a place lecturing at your university on the volcanoes of Mexico!'

By the time Ron and Jim left the truck, the driver had a pocket full of information about the Parícutin and some tracts that told him about his need for Jesus as Saviour. During all their lifts on the long trip south to Mexico, Ron and Jim gave out tracts to the people with whom they came into conversation.

'That's one of the good things about hitchhiking,' Jim commented, as they stood waiting at a junction for a lift. 'We are able to talk about the Lord to people we'd never meet otherwise.'

'How much Spanish do you think you can learn in six weeks?' Ron asked, seeing Jim writing in his notebook. 'There's no exam before you're allowed to go home.'

His friend laughed. 'Say that again … in Spanish!'

The language was no problem to Ron Harris, whose parents had come out to Mexico from England as missionaries several years before. He moved between English and Spanish almost without thinking.

'What are these flowers called in Spanish?' Jim asked.

Ron told him, and his friend wrote the word in the fourth of five lists in his book.

'If that's your list of Spanish flower names, what are the other four lists for?'

'The first is for birds, the second for trees, the third one is the names of the hills and mountains around here and the last one is the streams and rivers.'

'You're certainly making an effort,' Ron laughed. 'If God calls you to work here in Mexico, you'll come with a head start...'

One evening, during a meeting, those gathered began to say the Lord's Prayer. Suddenly Ron was aware of a voice at his side. It was Jim speaking softly, along with the others in church.

Padre nuestro que estás en los cielos,
santificado sea tu nombre.
Venga tu reino.
Hágase tu voluntad, como en el cielo, así también en la tierra.
El pan nuestro de cada día, dánoslo hoy.
Y pérdonanos nuestras deudas,
como también nosotros perdonamos a nuestros deudores.
Y nos metas en tentación, mas líbranos del mal.
Porque tuyo es el reino, y el poder y la gloria,
por todos los siglos. Amén.

'You really have been working at the language,' Ron said, as they left the service. 'Who taught you the Lord's Prayer?'

'I asked one of the children,' admitted Jim. 'They're the best teachers of all!'

Two weeks after they arrived in Mexico, Jim wrote home to his parents.

'Mexico has stolen my heart. We've been here a fortnight (as Ron's parents say; they are very English) and they have invited me to stay for as long as I wish. Right now I almost wish it were for life. The Lord has been good to me in bringing me here and giving me this brief opportunity to see the work and hear the language a bit. Missionaries are very human folks, just doing what they are asked. They're simply a bunch of nobodies trying to exalt Somebody.'

As Jim signed his letter, he thought about the last sentence he had written. Was it true, he wondered, that he was happy to be a nobody? Did it matter to him that he'd never be famous or rich or important? Did it matter to him that he might never marry, never have children, never be a somebody in this world? And he knew in his heart, that the Somebody who meant everything to him was Jesus. And if Jim Elliot could, by being a nobody, lead people to Jesus, he was willing to do that. And he would count it a privilege.

'This has been an amazing six weeks,' Jim told Mr Harris, not long before he was due to leave for home. 'I've learned such a lot.'

'I know that,' the missionary said. 'And I'm impressed by the amount of Spanish you've managed to cram into your brain in such a short time. However, I wonder if you would speak to the children before you leave. But perhaps you'd better use an interpreter for that. Six weeks of Spanish isn't quite up to giving a children's talk!'

Jim agreed to do the talk, and said he would think about using an interpreter. In the end, he decided to tell the children about Noah's ark and the rainbow of promise.

'I'll give the talk without an interpreter,' he decided, and told Mr Harris.

'Are you sure? What happens if you run out of words?' the missionary asked.

'If I can have the use of a blackboard, the children will help me out.'

Mr Harris arranged for the blackboard and waited to see how his son's friend would do.

'Boys and girls, today I'm going to tell you the story of Noah and the ark God asked him to build,' Jim began in Spanish, much to the children's surprise.

They knew he could hardly speak any Spanish. After all, he'd being going around for a whole six weeks asking the words for perfectly ordinary things!

'When God looked at the world he had made, he saw men, women and children doing everything evil. There was just one good man, and his name was Noah. He had three sons: Shem, Ham and Japheth.'

The children were amazed at how well Jim was doing, though he did make some funny mistakes that made them smile.

'So God said to Noah, "I'm going to put an end to all the people …"'

The story went on until, suddenly, Jim did not know a word.

He had just said, 'Make a …..' when he stopped, grabbed a piece of chalk and drew a house on the blackboard. Jim then pointed at the roof, and the children told him what the word was in Spanish. As though nothing at all had happened, the young man continued with the story.

'God said to Noah, "Make a roof for the ark. Put a door

in the side of the ark and make lower, middle and upper decks.'"

Occasionally during the story of Noah and the rainbow of promise, Jim came across a word he didn't know. Each time he did a drawing on the blackboard and the children told him the word he was looking for. By the end of the story the blackboard was covered with drawings of a house with its roof, of a raven and an elephant, of a branch, two snakes and numerous other things as well. And when the long story ended, the children were so taken with the work Jim had put into the lesson, that they learned the memory verse in record quick time.

'Say it after me,' Jim told them.

And they did, five … six … seven times.

He congratulated them on doing so well. 'Now say it yourselves.'

'Mientras el mundo exista,' they said together, 'habrá siembra y cosecha; hará calor y frío, habrá invierno y verano y días con sus noches.'

'Now, boys and girls, would you like to hear that in my language.'

The children nodded their heads. They were delighted with their new teacher. He was certainly very different!

'This is the promise God made to Noah,' Jim explained, in Spanish. Then, switching to English, he said;

'As long as the earth endures, seedtime and harvest, cold and heat, summer and winter, day and night will never cease' (Genesis 8 verse 22),

'Will you all remember it?' he asked, in Spanish.

And Jim knew from their smiling faces that they would.

Elisabeth

Back at Wheaton for a third year, Jim found himself sitting opposite a student called Elisabeth Howard. He had noticed her around, and he knew her brother, Dave.

'Jim Elliot looks like a wrestler, all right,' Elisabeth thought. 'Just under 6 feet tall, he has the bull neck and barrel chest I would have expected. His grey-blue eyes suit the sky-coloured sweater he wears most of the time, along with his grey trousers and slightly shabby jacket. And his socks and ties usually match.'

A week or two after the beginning of term, Jim asked the girl across the aisle if she would go out with him on a date.

'That would be lovely, thanks,' she said.

But before the day for the date came round, Elisabeth spoke to Jim and cancelled it.

'Why did you do that?' her friend gasped. 'Don't you know that he never asks a girl out? You've blown your chances with Jim Elliot! That was a really stupid move.'

Elisabeth was left in absolutely no doubt what her friends thought of what she'd done! However, they were a little more hopeful for her when Jim accepted Dave's invitation to spend Christmas in the Howard home.

'This is new country to me,' Jim said, as they prepared to travel east through the December landscape.

'And it's lovely country,' Elisabeth assured him. 'First we go due east to Toledo. From there we go along the southern shore of Lake Erie, then through Pennsylvania and over the Allegheny mountains then the Appalachians before dropping down to New Jersey.'

'They're really all part of the Appalachians, but it does seem like two mountain ranges when you're travelling through them,' explained Dave.

'Where are the highest peaks, and what height are they?' Jim wondered.

'The Alleghenies are highest in the south, some of them reaching 4000 feet,' Dave told him. 'In the north the highest is about half of that.'

'And the Appalachians?' asked Jim.

'They're much higher,' Elisabeth said. 'I think Mt Mitchell is over 6680 feet high.'

'I don't suppose there's much chance of us climbing Mt Mitchell in December then?' asked Jim, half-hopefully.

Elisabeth laughed. 'No, there is not. Absolutely none at all!'

Jim was very warmly welcomed into the Howard family as his first letter home, written just four days before Christmas, makes clear.

'Here I am in the midst of a fine family: a fellow Bob's age and his wife; then there is Elisabeth, who is 21 today and a senior at Wheaton; she is followed by brother Dave. Below him are Ginny, a bobby-soxer of 15 who closes her eyes like Jane when she grins, which she does much; and Tommy, 13; with Jimmy, aged 7, who combine to keep the rest of us in fine spirits and good humour. Again I find God's people very good, and this family is particularly godly.'

But though he felt welcome in their home, Jim was a little less comfortable in church. It wasn't that he disagreed with anything, or that people didn't greet him warmly, it was just that the form of the service was not familiar to him. He had been brought up in the Plymouth Brethren while the Howards were members of another denomination.

'What a nice young man Master Dave and Miss Elisabeth brought home with them,' the little old lady, who helped in the house, told Mrs Howard. 'He's been giving me a hand to dry the dishes today. That young man will go places,' she went on. 'When he finds a fork that's not well washed, he washes it again himself, instead of asking me to do it.' Then she grinned. 'And even though I'm getting deaf, I can hear that boy singing.' Mrs Howard raised her eyebrows. 'Yes,' the old lady smiled. 'He sings while we do the dishes, and he has such a good clear voice that my deaf old ears can hear him. And he doesn't need to sing the same hymn twice, for I think he knows hundreds of them!'

'May I clear the snow for you?' Jim asked Mr Howard, when he arrived in the kitchen early one morning just as his host was pulling on his boots.

Mr Howard looked up and smiled. 'That's a mighty fine offer to make, and I accept it gladly.'

Minutes later, Jim was outside shovelling snow for all he was worth. Yet he still had the breath to sing as he worked. Perhaps those who were inside and asleep didn't appreciate his musical efforts first thing in the morning!

'Do you like sledging?' Jim asked Ginny and Tommy one afternoon, after a particularly fine fall of snow.

'We sure do!' Ginny laughed. 'Are you offering to come with us?'

Jim grinned. 'Try to stop me!'

The three of them set off, pulling sledges behind them. By then Jim was 20 years old, but he could enjoy sledging like a schoolboy! He lay on his stomach on the sledge and careered down the hillside at break-neck speed … but succeeded in not breaking his neck. And the following day, when he took the two teenagers ice-skating, he managed not to break anything – with the possible exception of the speed limit on ice. The Howard young people were discovering that their visitor was quite an athlete, and very fit indeed.

After family worship, the Howards headed for bed, apart from Elisabeth who stayed up to chat with Jim.

'Goodness me!' she laughed, after they had talked late into their last night before going back to Wheaton. 'I don't know where the time has gone these evenings when we've sat up chatting. And the subjects we've discussed!'

'We just tackled one or two,' teased Jim. 'There was poetry, women, the church, parts of the Bible, to name but a few. We still have a great deal of talking to do.'

'Maybe so,' Elisabeth yawned. 'But not tonight. I'm shattered.'

She rose to her feet and was about to leave the room, when she turned round and grinned at her friend.

'I really enjoy our conversations, even when we disagree.'

Jim shrugged his shoulders. 'There should be room for disagreements,' he said, 'provided they don't turn into arguments. Arguing is never a good start to a night's sleep.'

'Goodnight,' said Elisabeth. 'Sleep well.'

'And you.'

Back in Wheaton, the days were full of studying, preparing for lectures and reading the books on their booklists. Although Jim had decided to remain single unless God showed him he should marry, that didn't stop him seeking out Elisabeth from time to time, though perhaps occasionally there was an ulterior motive.

'Jim has discovered that I always do my Greek assignment at a certain table in the hall,' Elisabeth told a friend. 'He's started joining me there quite regularly. Mind you, there are moments when I'm a little suspicious that I'm doing most of the work.'

Her friend smiled. She knew Elisabeth was good at Greek.

'But what does it matter, we get through the passages more quickly when we do them together.'

Although Jim and Elisabeth saw each other in College, they never went out on a date together.

Getting through work quickly was important to Jim Elliot, especially as he had set himself a strict programme of Bible reading.

'How do you fit it all in?' Pete Fleming, his roommate, asked.

'I've worked out a timetable that works for me,' explained Jim. 'You know I spend an hour reading the Bible in the morning before breakfast.'

Pete nodded.

'I just read the Old Testament during that hour,' Jim said. 'Then at lunchtime I find a few minutes to read and think about one of the psalms. And in the evening I read from the New Testament.'

'I see you've bought yourself a new Bible,' Pete

observed. 'Could you not read your old one because you had underlined so many verses and written so much in the margins?'

Jim grinned. 'You're nearly right! I discovered that when I read parts of the Bible I'd read before, I paid more attention to the comments I'd written previously than to the Word of God. So my new Bible is not going to have anything written on it, or any verses underlined. The whole Bible is the Word of God, and I'm going to try to see each verse as being important rather than just my favourite ones.'

'You organise your prayer life very carefully too, don't you?' asked Pete.

'I try to,' agreed Jim. 'Otherwise I'd promise to pray for someone and never do it. I have a list of people for each day of the week, and I pray for them on that day. When there's someone else I want to pray for, I add him to one of the daily lists then I know I'll pray for him every week.'

'I've copied your little text cards,' Pete told his friend. 'It's a really good idea to write verses on small cards and keep them in your pocket to read and learn when you have just a minute to spare. Since I started doing that, I've discovered just how many times in the day I do have a minute or two to spare.'

'The only problem I've found with them,' Jim admitted, 'is that people occasionally think I'm being antisocial, because I'd rather learn a verse from the Bible than chat to them about nothing in particular.'

'You'll have to watch that,' Pete pointed out. 'Because sometimes when you meet people casually, you have the chance to talk to them about Jesus after you've discussed the day's football results.'

'I'll try not to disturb you if you're asleep when I come in,' Jim told Pete, the following night.

Pete grinned. 'If you wake me up I'll throw my pillow at you – and put a brick inside it first. What's going to be keeping you so late tonight?'

'Just packing parcels. A whole lot of stuff is ready to go off to Europe. It just needs to be packed and wrapped up.'

His friend screwed up his face.

'I suppose if I came and helped you it would be done in half the time, and that would mean you could get to bed earlier,' said Pete.

'Which,' Jim laughed, 'would have the distinct advantage that I wouldn't risk being hit by a brick-filled pillow!'

Americans knew that people in Europe were still short of many food items, even through the Second World War had finished two years before. Many organisations collected food and other things, and these were parcelled up and dispatched as relief packages to Britain and Europe. The only time Jim had free to become involved was late at night, and he was glad of Pete's help from time to time.

Jim's Sunday afternoons were not spent lounging in the sun between services. Very often he took himself into one or another of Chicago's main railway stations where he talked to those who were hanging around waiting for trains.

'How do you begin a Christian conversation with a stranger on a railway platform?' someone asked him, one day. 'Is it not embarrassing?'

Jim looked at his fellow student.

'Jesus Christ died on the cross so that my sins could

be forgiven and so that I will go home to him in heaven when I die, or when he comes again,' said Jim Elliot very seriously. 'Do you think he was embarrassed bearing my sins on the cross?'

His friend didn't know what to say.

'And I will not be embarrassed to talk to strangers about the One who can be their Saviour. It's the best news in the whole wide world, the best news there ever has been or ever will be. And until everyone has heard it, I will keep on speaking to people I know, and people I don't know, about Jesus.'

In April 1948, Jim and some of his friends were travelling as a gospel team to speak at a meeting.

'There's something wrong with the car,' the driver said, as it spluttered to a stop.

He turned the key frantically trying to bring the engine back to life again.

'We're right in the middle of a level crossing!' yelled one of the students in the back seat. 'Get out the car!'

The doors were shoved open and all the students scrambled out – only just in time – as a freight train smashed into their car a few seconds later.

Standing at the side of the railway track, the gospel team looked at what was left of the car, and realised just how little would have been left of them had God not helped them to get out super-fast. The side of a level crossing is not the usual place for a prayer meeting, but there was one held there that day. And all the prayers were the same. 'Thank you, thank you, dear Father in heaven, thank you.'

Elisabeth Howard graduated from Wheaton in 1948. Towards the end of her last term, she and Jim went for a walk one evening to discuss their future. It was almost a surprise to them when they had to admit they were in love. But there was something even more serious than that they had to discuss. Did God mean them to marry? They agreed to wait until they were absolutely sure that he did. And if God did not mean them to marry, they would not.

'Look at that,' Jim said, quietly, as they sat together in a dark and silent cemetery.

The moon had come out, and it cast a shadow of a large stone cross between them.

Graduation and Beyond

'What are you doing this summer?' a Wheaton student asked Jim, in June 1948.

'Four of us are heading off as a gospel team to speak at meetings right through the Midwestern States,' was the reply.

His friend laughed. 'That's not much of a holiday, at least it's not my idea of a holiday.'

Jim looked at him. 'There are more worthwhile things to do than lounge around in the sun. And I'd rather spend my summer talking about Jesus than anything else.'

'I'll hear about it in the autumn,' the other student said, 'when I come back refreshed and you return in need of a holiday!'

Jim and his friend Dave (Elisabeth's brother), Roger and Verd, set off in July for their hard-working holiday. They travelled north from Wheaton, through Wisconsin to Minnesota, speaking to groups all along the way. In mid August they headed for Red Lake, Minnesota.

'Why's the lake called Red Lake,' one of the boys asked, as they travelled.

Jim had read up about the community there, and was able to give him an answer.

'About 1750, the Chippewa people arrived there from the Great Lakes. The earliest map that shows the name Red Lake dates from five years later, and the words are written in French. But the Indian name for the lake is Miskwagamiwizaga-iganing, and that also means Red Lake. It's reckoned the name comes from the colour of the lake when it reflects the setting sun.'

'The Indian people have a sad history,' sighed Dave.

Jim opened up a book on the subject, and filled his friends in on the history of the people to whom they were going to speak about Jesus.

'The last Sioux withdrew from the area in 1765 after a battle with the Ponemah Indians. The fur trade was established in the area after that.'

'When did missionaries first come?' Dave asked.

'There was a Protestant mission at Red Lake in 1842,' Jim said, having flicked through the pages to find the answer. 'But it only lasted 15 years before the missionaries withdrew. It doesn't say why. Do you want to know any more?' Jim enquired.

'Sure,' said Dave. 'What else do you know?'

Consulting the book again, Jim said, 'There are four reservation communities: Red Lake Village, Redby, Ponemah and Little Rock. And it seems that this reservation is different from any others, as the Indian people here run the place through hereditary chiefs. The federal government is only involved if major crimes are committed.'

'Glad to have an opportunity to preach the gospel … to stoical pagan Indians. What a privilege to be made a minister of the 'happy God', Jim wrote in his journal, soon afterwards. 'I only hope that he will let me preach to those who have never heard the name of Jesus.'

From Red Lake they travelled westwards, climbing higher as they journeyed on, because their route took them over the Rocky Mountains.

'We'll come to the Continental Divide before long,' commented Roger. 'Look out for the first river running westwards.'

'It's a strange thing to have a imaginary line running along the crest of the Rockies from British Columbia in the north right down to Mexico, with rivers on one side of it running to the east, and rivers on the other side of it all running to the west into the Pacific,' Jim said, as he watched for the change in water direction.

He watched until his eyes grew tired. Their programme of meetings was heavy, and the more he watched the more heavy his eyelids became. Suddenly Jim woke with a jolt.

'Did I sleep long?' he asked, stretching himself as far as space allowed.

'Not long,' Dave assured him. 'But long enough to miss the Continental Divide. Look!' he said, pointing out the window. 'The river is flowing west towards the Pacific.'

'Would you believe it?' laughed Jim. 'I watch so hard for the watershed that I fall asleep and miss it!'

When Jim Elliot went back to Wheaton in September 1948, for his final year there, Elisabeth moved to Canada to do missionary work in countryside communities. They continued to pray that God would show them his plans for their future, and make clear to them whether that included them being married or not.

8th October 1948
'This is my 21st birthday,' Jim wrote. 'Yesterday I prayed that God would take me to Peru or Brazil before I pass another October 8th.'

On that day he was looking forward. A month later, when he spoke to a fellow student who was having doubts

He is No Fool
about the truth of the Bible, Jim remembered back to when he became a Christian. 'I wasn't "saved" all at once,' he said. 'It took some years before I was sure about the truth of God.'

That fact helped him in his discussions with people who were still trying to work out what they believed. 'If it took me years,' he concluded, 'why do I expect others to trust in the Lord Jesus all at once.'

'Sometimes that happens, and it is wonderful when it does,' a friend commented, as they discussed the matter. 'But God deals with different people in different ways.'

Although Jim was coming to the end of his studies, and had a great deal of work to do, he still found time for wrestling.

'We lost our first wresting meet to Illinois Norman today,' he wrote home, just before Christmas. 'That was quite a blow, since it's the first time they've beaten us in remembered history, and we're supposed to be an experienced team. I took my match by a decision of 14 points to 3, but couldn't seem to pin the guy. However, it sure was fun and it keeps me fit too!'

For some time, Jim thought that the Lord wanted him to go as a missionary either to India or to South America. But how was he to decide between them? He prayed, he listened to what others said, and he waited for God to show him the right direction.

'I'm so glad I came,' Jim told a friend, at the International Student Missionary Convention in the University of Illinois, at the end of that year.

His friend asked why that was.

96

'Being here has helped me to decide where God wants me to go. I now feel that tribal work in the South American jungle is what he is asking me to do, and I am confident that he wants me to begin the work still single.'

'What about Elisabeth?' his friend asked.

'I'll write to her,' said Jim. 'She'll understand that we cannot begin to think about marriage for some years yet. Elisabeth wants to do God's will just as much as I do.'

Jim wrote, and the pair of them decided that they would go on writing to each other, and trusting each other to the Lord's care.

The Elliots had not only bred one son for the mission field, Jim's brother Bert, who was just about to be married, had felt the Lord's call to work in Peru. Jim went home for the wedding in January 1949, and that was the last time ever that his family was to be together until the day when they will all meet again in heaven. Bert and his bride, Colleen, left Portland soon after their wedding to travel south to Peru.

'What's The 49-er's Centennial Day and their Annual Reverse Day,' Jane asked her mother, when Jim's letter came in describing it.

Mum Elliot shook her head. 'It's an excuse for fun and games, and special for Jim's class because they graduate this year, 1949. They dress us as though they were students a hundred years ago.'

'Look what he says!' laughed Jane.

'Read it to me,' Mum Elliot asked, her hands being covered in bread flour.

Jane perched on a ledge beside the sink and read what her brother had written.

'Reverse Day is when the girls date the fellows, opening doors for them, and generally behaving like the gentlemen we usually are! I borrowed Uncle's most old-fashioned clothes: spats, top hat, stiff collar with wings, bow tie, tail coat, the lot! The girls wore hoop skirts, bustles and piled their hair up as it would have been in 1849.'

'I can just picture him!' said Mum Elliot. 'He'd look like his great-grandfather! What else does he say?'

'I even had a walking stick with a carved dog's head and built-in gun chamber! And ... I was presented with a tie for growing a beard for three weeks!'

'A beard!' laughed Mum Elliot. 'Your brother is quite extraordinary!'

Jane giggled at the thought.

Soon afterwards a letter arrived telling them that he'd had his beard cut off.

'Thank goodness for that,' Dad Elliot said.

Jane grinned. 'I hope he had his photograph taken with his beard. I'd love to see it.'

'He must be very busy,' her father said, when he read Jim's letter. 'He's not even had time to classify and mount the stamps we sent him.'

'Stamp collecting is a good hobby,' commented Jane. 'You can do it when you have time, and lay it aside for months when you're busy.'

Busy or not, where there are students there is always time for fun and games. When Ed McCully, who was in Jim's year at Wheaton, won a national public speaking competition in San Francisco, his friends – Jim included – congratulated him by throwing him in the lake when he returned back home to College!

Just when Jim was wondering what he should do after he graduated from Wheaton, a letter came from his brother telling him that he was about to start building a house for himself and his wife. 'Would you be interested in helping with the building work?' Bob asked.

'I'm sure three months of building work will be great experience for missionary service,' Jim told Ed, when they discussed it.

'That's certainly true,' Ed agreed. 'Have you noticed how often missionaries tell us about building their own homes and places in which to hold services?'

In fact, Jim had come to the conclusion that he should spend a year back home – after all, he'd been away in Wheaton for four years. He knew there was plenty to keep him busy, preaching in his local assembly (that's what a Plymouth Brethren group is called), maintaining the Assembly Hall that needed a great deal of work done on it, perhaps school teaching too.

'I'll cram the year full of experiences that will help me in my mission work.'

'Is the scaffolding secure?' Dad Elliot asked his son, when they'd tightened the last bolt.

Jim reached up, grabbed a crossbar, felt it for strength then swung from it.

'It's secure all right,' he said. 'You have a break and I'll put up the pulleys.'

The pair of them were about to start painting the hall in which their Brethren Assembly met. It was a dry day, just right for the job.

Jim climbed up the ladder with two pulley wheels in his hand. Fixing them to the top bar of the scaffolding wasn't a problem. Then he ran a rope through each of them and lowered the ends to his father, who was shading his eyes from the sun in order to see what Jim was doing.

'Did you learn all you need to be a missionary at College then?' his father asked, as they worked together.

Jim knew the answer to that, but he thought hard before putting it into words.

'No,' he said. 'I learned a lot, but I think you need to do the work to really learn how to do it well. For example, my six weeks in Mexico taught me more than months at College.'

'So you're saying that you would learn better working with an experienced man, just as Paul trained Barnabas in the Bible?' Dad Elliot asked.

'That exactly right!' agreed Jim. 'That's the kind of experience I need to get.'

'Well, there's plenty of it to be had hereabouts,' his father assured him. 'And you can join me on my preaching trips too.'

'This year could be really valuable then,' Jim thought. 'There's so much more I still need to know and learn.'

Some weeks later, Jim turned over the pages of his journal to that day's date, October 28th 1949. He thought for a while before beginning to write, and when he put pen to paper it was to write only two sentences. 'One of the greatest blessings of heaven is the appreciation of heaven on earth. He is no fool who gives what he cannot keep to gain what he cannot lose.'

The words played on his mind all day. And late in the evening, when his mother asked him what he was thinking, Jim repeated some of the words he had written. 'He is no fool who gives what he cannot keep to gain what he cannot lose.'

Mum Elliot thought about what her son had said. 'That's so true,' she agreed, putting her hand on his shoulder. 'We cannot keep our lives, so we give them to the Lord to do with as he pleases. And what do we gain? We gain the hope of one day being in heaven with him. And we can never lose that, for nobody and nothing can take it away from us.'

'I couldn't have put it better myself,' said Jim quietly. 'And I have given my life to the Lord. I just wonder what he will do with it between here and heaven.'

The Waiting Time

'Right,' Jim said firmly to himself, 'how am I going to get through today?'

He had just finished his usual morning time of Bible reading and prayer, and the last thing he asked the Lord was for strength and wisdom to cope with the day. He would need it. Not only was his diary full for that day, it was full for the whole week!

'Onwards and upwards,' he grinned. 'I'll not do anything if I just sit here thinking about it.'

But when evening came, he did sit for a while and think about it.

'Some people seem to be of the opinion that I'm doing nothing,' he worried. 'Today I went to the Christian School to apply for a job as a substitute teacher. Then I studied for most of the day. After that there was the party ....' He broke into a wide smile as memories of the party tumbled into his head.

'You look like a dog with a juicy bone,' his father said, as he sat down on the other side of the fire. 'I take it this evening went well.'

His son nodded. 'You could say that.'

'And are you going to tell me about it, or do I have to force each bit of information from you like a dentist pulling teeth?'

Laughing at his father's joke, Jim lay back in the chair, stretched his legs out in front of the fire, and told Dad Elliot about his visit to the local detention home for boys.

'Well, I was invited to go as part of the entertainment for their party. And, as I'm not really a stand-up comic, I decided to tell them a mystery story by Edgar Allen Poe. When I was young, you often pulled me up on your knee to tell me a story. And I was so big by the time Jane was old enough to take my place on your knee, that you must have been in pain with the weight of me! But, Dad, I felt that many of the boys in the detention home had never been told a story in their lives. They didn't know how to sit, or how to listen. But I chose a story in which the tension builds quickly, and within a couple of minutes they were sitting wide-eyed and open-mouthed waiting for the next thing to happen. And when the story reached its climax, most of them held their breath while I dangled them over a barrel of suspense. And you should have seen their faces when the mystery untangled itself! I could feel the relief in the room. One of the boys told me that I sure know how to tell a story. Of course, that opened the way for me to tell them a story about the Lord.'

'I hope they listened as carefully to that one,' said Dad Elliot.

'They did,' Jim assured him. 'And they would have sat all night listening to stories had time not run out.'

The following evening, it was a Tuesday, Jim was surrounded by children once again, this time at an Assembly meeting-place in the outskirts of Portland. And he, and the little group of boys round about him, were absolutely engrossed in what they were doing. Some were cutting squares of white linen to a pattern Jim had given them. Others were measuring fine twisted thread for rigging. Two boys held fiddly bits of wood together until the glue they had applied was firmly set.

'Do you know anything about this kind of boat?' Stephen asked.

'Do I!' laughed Jim. 'You are talking to a serious maker of model sailing ships, my lad!'

Stephen grinned. He didn't know why, but he just loved coming to this club. His parents thought he was odd. Why did he want to go to a Christian club? That was for little girls and old women! But Stephen, and the other children who attended the Assembly's club, were given such interesting things to do that they kept coming back. And each time they came, they learned something more about the Lord Jesus Christ.

'This splendid sailing ship,' said Jim, holding up the picture on the outside of the model box, is The Sovereign of the Seas. She was built in 1638. The builder's name was Phineas Pett, and the ship was built for King Charles 1 of Great Britain. She was the biggest ship on the seas at the time, the biggest by far. The Sovereign of the Seas carried 100 guns, and was the first British ship to take a member of the Royal family as a passenger. What else would you like to know?' he asked.

Stephen, who was fascinated with small details, wanted to know her exact specifications.

'The ship was 212 feet long, 48 feet wide at the beam and 19 ¼ feet deep. Her tonnage was 1605, and she worked on a wartime crew of 815 men.'

'How do you remember all that?' Stephen asked.

Jim grinned. 'You just plugged into one of my favourite hobbies!'

'What else can you tell us about The Sovereign of the Sea?' queried the boy.

Jim, who knew it was time to pack up for the evening, gave them just enough information to make them want to come back the following week for more.

'I'll tell you three more things about her. One, all her carvings were finished in real gold leaf. Two, the Dutch called her The Golden Devil. Three, she was one of the first ships to have all her windows made of glass.'

'Tell us more about the ship?' Stephen pleaded.

'I'll tell you about another boat instead,' said Jim. And the children all fell silent as he told them about a terrible storm in the Sea of Galilee, a storm in which experienced sailors were so afraid they thought they were going to drown.

'But there was one man in the boat who wasn't in the least concerned about the storm. In fact, he was sound asleep,' Jim told them 'His name was Jesus. His friends were so terrified that they wakened him out of his sleep and accused him of not caring what happened to them.'

'Did they drown?' Stephen asked.

Jim went on with the story. 'Jesus stood up in the boat, and commanded the wind to stop blowing and the waves to stop roaring.'

Stephen's eyes were wide open. 'What happened then?' he asked.

Jim smiled. 'The wind stopped blowing, of course. And the sea stopped raging.'

'How did that happen?' the children wanted to know.

Their friend explained. 'Jesus made the wind and the sea, and they obey him when he tells them what to do.'

'Phew!' breathed Stephen. 'My dad says this club is for wimps, but that's not a wimp's story! I'll tell him it when I get home. He likes sea stories.'

On Wednesday Jim was back among children again, this time in his own Assembly. They just loved having him home. He seemed to have so much more time than other adults to get to know them and to discuss things with them. Nearly all of Thursday was spent studying, as well as preparing for talks he had to give over the weekend. Then on Friday, he went to a local business where he took a service for the people who worked there. It was Saturday evening before Jim and his father had much time to talk again.

'Are you tired, Son?' Dad Elliot asked.

Jim grinned. 'I'm too young to be tired by a busy week,' he said. 'But do you know what does tire me?'

His father wondered what was coming.

'Some people, even some of those in our Assembly, seem to think that I should be away in the jungle somewhere preaching to people who have never heard about Jesus. I get the impression that they think I'm just lazing around and wasting my time here. But I don't feel it's right for me to go to the mission field quite yet. And I do feel I'm doing worthwhile work right here.'

Jim's dad sighed. He'd also heard what some people had been saying.

'Tell me,' said Dad Elliot, 'is it more important to you to please God and do what you believe he wants you to do, or to please men and do what you think they want you to do.'

'There's no contest,' the young man said. 'My heart is the Lord's, and my aim in life is to please him.'

'In that case,' his father advised him, 'take no heed of what people say. One day God may show them the value of the work you're doing just now. But even if he does not, what's important is that you do what the Saviour tells you to do.'

While Jim worked in a whole variety of ways, he still looked forward to the day when God would lead him away from home to some distant place as a missionary. Elisabeth also waited on the Lord's guidance, as she worked as a rural missionary in Canada. Letters went between them regularly and, no doubt, both also waited to see if the Lord would one day open the way for them to become man and wife.

One letter Jim wrote to Elisabeth shows the direction – and also the uncertainty – of his thinking. 'I have had detailed correspondence with two missionaries to whom I wrote; one, Wilfred Tidmarsh of Ecuador (whose wife was injured in a Missionary Aviation Fellowship plane crash when Nate Saint was pilot), who is having to leave an established forest work among Quichua Indians for a while; the other Rowland Hill of Bangalore, India. Both describe fields of tremendous interest to me, and both are quite anxious regarding my leading from the Lord. From one standpoint the works are almost opposite, as the Ecuadorian work is among primitive unlettered tribes-people, while the Indian project is among high school and collage-age upper class Hindus who are studying English. Brother Hill wants to start a Bible school for some of them, and is looking for someone who would qualify as a teacher of Greek, etc., as well as working in the wide-open schools. How is one to decide when the heart is equally torn for both works, and one's capabilities fit either sphere?'

Three weeks later, as Jim thought about Elisabeth, a children's rhyme came into his head.

'Peter, Peter Pumpkin eater
had a wife and could not keep her.

He put her in a pumpkin shell,
and there he kept her very well.

A broad smile lit up his face, then faded. 'That's exactly
what life is like,' he thought. 'If I am to marry Elisabeth,
I'll have to be like Peter and find a place to keep her. And
as most wives wouldn't be happy living in a pumpkin shell,
I would need to find a house for her. And a house needs
curtains, rugs, a washing machine etc. When it's full of all
it needs, it becomes a home. And a home is for children.'
Jim's thinking continued along these lines, as though he
was unravelling a puzzle. 'Children need to be taken places
by car, and a car requires a garage. You need land on which
to build a garage, and land needs looking after to make
it a garden. Then a garden needs tools and the tools need
sharpening!' As he thought about it, there seemed to be
no end of things that would be needed if he were to marry
the girl he loved. 'It's all too complicated,' he decided. 'For
the time being, it is very much simpler for us both to stay
single.'

One day, in January 1950, Jim decided to spend a little
while sorting through the stamps he had collected, but
which he'd not had time to sort and mount. 'I'll only do
it for an hour,' he decided. But at the end of the hour he
was still sorting though the American stamps that had been
printed since he'd last had time to work on them. Picking
them up one by one, each seemed to bring a memory of his
past into his mind.

'Look at that,' Jim smiled to himself, as he held a 1946
US Air mail 5-cent stamp that depicted a Skymaster in
flight. 'That takes me right back to my model plane days!'

He picked up a 1947 3-cent stamp, with a picture of the US sailing frigate Constitution on it. 'Well, well!' he grinned. 'There's Old Ironsides herself!' Then he laughed aloud. He has just noticed a 1949 stamp with a picture of Edgar Allen Poe, and Jim remembered back to his evening telling Poe's mystery stories to the boys in the detention home. How carefully they had listened. And the thought brought a great yearning into Jim's heart. He longed to tell stories of Jesus to people who had never even heard his name before. 'Look at the time!' he gasped. 'I've spent ages on these stamps, much longer than I intended to.'

As Jim packed his stamps away till another day, one slid away from the others. Picking it up carefully, the picture on it caught his attention. It showed the Wright brothers with an early aeroplane. 'That came out last year to mark the 75th anniversary of their first flight,' Jim remembered. As he looked at the stamp his mind wandered in the skies. He imagined himself in a plane that was about to land where God wanted him to be a missionary. But however hard he looked out of the aeroplane window, he could not see what country he was about to land in.

Six months later, Jim was at the University of Oklahoma, along with hundreds of missionaries, or people who thought that the Lord might be leading them to be missionaries. And they were not there for a holiday.

'This is fascinating stuff,' Jim told a fellow student. 'I'd not realised how much is involved in writing down an unwritten language. It's a case of studying and analysing sounds, accents, tones, just everything to do with how words are spoken.'

'That's right,' his friend said. 'But I'm a bit scared about the assignment we've to do.'

Jim grinned. 'I'm looking forward to it! What a great opportunity to have an experienced missionary go through the whole process of collecting and organising language data with us!'

'It's not so hard for you,' the other young man laughed. 'You're such a good mimic that you pick up sounds well. I've got to listen so hard that my brain is exhausted within the hour and I feel as if my ears are falling off the sides of my head!'

The missionary with whom Jim was to study had worked with the Quichuas in the jungles of Ecuador. As they worked together, Jim's heart warmed to the Quichua people, and his pulse raced when his missionary mentor told him about a tribe in Ecuador who were not only untouched by the gospel, but they were also untouched by civilisation.

'They are the Aucas,' the missionary said. 'And no one has penetrated their communities with the good news of Jesus.'

'What are they like?' Jim asked, his pioneer heart stirring at the thought of a truly unreached people.

The missionary shook his head. 'They are the most cruel of people,' he said. 'And the most in need of Jesus.'

Remembering the correspondence he had had with Dr Tidmarsh, Jim thought long and hard about Ecuador. He thought of the Quichua people and of the Aucas. Could it be just a coincidence that the missionary with whom he had studied had worked in Ecuador, the same country in which Dr Tidmarsh served? Jim, who was used to seeing God working through circumstances, did not think it was.

He decided to dedicate ten days to praying about his future. At the end of the ten days, he knew in his heart that God wanted him to work in Ecuador. Not long after his course in Oklahoma ended, Jim wrote in his journal what had to be done next. First, he was going to ask God for another young man who would go to Eastern Ecuador with him. Second, he had to learn Spanish and Quichua. Third, he and the other young man would have to get to know each other. Fourth, they would have to learn how God wanted them to approach the Quichua peoples who lived in the Ecuadorian highlands.

Jim put his pen down. 'It's easy enough to write that,' he said to himself. 'But it won't be as easy to do it. The Quichuas need to be reached for God, and we can only do that with God's help.'

To Ecuador

The minute hand of the custom's house clock crept round past 2pm on 4th February 1952, but its ticking was drowned out by all the noise of the Outer Harbour Dock, San Pedro, California, as a ship prepared to sail. Jim Elliot and Pete Fleming stood at the rail of the *Santa Juana* waving to those on shore who had come to see them off.

Dad and Mum Elliot stood side by side on the pier as the long seconds ticked by. And at six minutes past the hour, the ship's horn sounded and the *Santa Juana* eased away from the quayside. Jim's prayer for God's guidance had been answered; he was on his way to Ecuador. And his prayer for someone to go with him was answered in the shape of his old friend Pete Fleming, with whom he had shared a room at Wheaton.

Their journey started calmly enough; but five days later, as they sailed through the Gulf of Tehauntepec, the wind was so strong that Jim was able to lean against it without falling over! While the journey was full of interest for the two young men, their main occupation was studying the Spanish language and using it with any crew member who had time to talk with them.

After 20 days on the *Santa Juana*, Jim and Pete transferred to the yacht *Santa Rosita* that took them into the port of Guayaquil where they passed through customs without a hitch – despite having twelve pieces of luggage weighing a total of 2,300 pounds! After an overnight stop in Guayaquil they caught the Panagra flight to Quito, where they were taken to a missionary family's home to stay until lodgings could be found for them with an Ecuadorian family. Spanish classes started right away.

'Quito is a beautiful, old, and picturesque city, lying between two mountain ranges,' Jim wrote home to his parents. 'Rhubarb was on our menu yesterday. Bananas, in all their forms, I'm beginning to get used to. So far we have had banana-meal mush for breakfast, fried bananas and raw ones too. A great bunch of green bananas is on the garage floor.'

In April, who should arrive in Quito but Elisabeth! She was to be there for some months studying Spanish, tropical diseases and other medical subjects. While all three worked very hard indeed, there was still some time for relaxing. During their study of tropical diseases with Dr Tidmarsh, the young people decided they would climb Pichincha on their first free day. Pete and Jim, with an American friend, their Ecuadorian 'right-hand-man' and Elisabeth, set off up the trail very early one morning.

'How high are we?' Pete asked, when they reached their final summit.

Jim told him that they were at 15,500 feet, the highest he had ever been on foot.

'Walking up through cascading water on both sides was magnificent,' said Elisabeth. 'And the variety of jutting peaks and rolling hills is quite extraordinary.'

The artist's eye in Jim had noted the exotic mountain flowers, some of them tiny, that grew in between slithers of rock where outcrops faced the sun.

By the end of July, Jim was sufficiently fluent in Spanish that he was able to preach at a morning service. And just a month later, after six months in Quito, the time came for the two young men to move on.

'We go to Shell Mera next Wednesday,' he told Elisabeth, knowing as he spoke that the months they had enjoyed living almost across the road from each other, were now about to come to an end. 'Pete and I will help in a boys' camp there before we move on to Shandia.'

'And I'll soon be leaving for the western foothills of the Andes to work with the Colorado Indians there,' Elisabeth said. 'It looks as though it's time to say goodbye once again.'

Jim and Elisabeth were in love, but both knew that the time had not come for them to marry. God still had work for them to do as single people.

'What do we do at camp?' Manuel asked, when he met Jim at the campsite. This was the boy's first camp, and he wanted to enjoy it to the full.

'Well,' said Jim. 'What have you done today so far?'

Manuel grinned. 'We were up at 6 am and had hot chocolate and bread rolls from a café. Then we sang choruses and learned some Bible verses. After that there was a Bible study and then we had to hunt through the Bible looking for what God says about us and about the Lord Jesus Christ. Will we be doing that all day?'

Jim smiled at the boy. 'No,' he assured him. 'I think there is something different planned for the rest of the day.'

They both tucked into their morning snack of sugar cane.

'Right, boys!' Pete shouted. 'Manuel, you be a captain. And you, Pedro, can captain the other team. Now, choose your teams for a game of football. Manuel, your team is the Quito Conquerors and, Pedro, you're captain of the Shell Mera Sharks!'

The game that followed was wild, and by the time Manuel collapsed in a heap beside Jim for lunch, he was high with excitement.

'You'll need your siesta,' Jim laughed, 'especially as we're going swimming in the stream just up the valley of the Pastaza later!'

Manuel wiped the perspiration off his forehead and stuffed some tostados into his mouth.

'Roasted corn kernels have never tasted so good, have they?' Jim laughed.

'Tostados,' Manuel corrected him.

Life was in serious Spanish now, and Jim had to remember it!

Two days later, Jim had just finished a Bible study with his little group of boys, when four of them began to sob. Their study had been on the Lord Jesus Christ, and the boys wanted to confess their sins and put their trust in him as their Saviour. That day those four boys became Christians.

'This is what mission work is all about,' Jim told Pete. 'And it's what makes all these hours of learning Spanish worthwhile.'

Camp over, it was time to move to Shandia, where Pete and Jim's work was to be based. Jim had to wait behind at Shell Mera for another plane, while Pete and Dr Tidmarsh went ahead. That night Jim wrote in his journal his feelings on arriving – at last – where he was to work as a missionary.

'Left Shell Mera at 3 pm in a sky of scattered clouds. Landed at Pano around 3.30, and made the walk to beautiful Shandia in just 2½ hours. The thought kept recurring as I came along the trail, "Right on time, right on time – God's time." My joy is full, full, full!'

'This is a truly amazing place,' said Jim, as he and Pete climbed down the fifty-five mud steps to have their daily swim in the Shandia River – that was their only bath!

'I'm glad we're beside the Shandia,' Pete laughed. 'After it flows into the Napo River the water is freezing cold!'

'That's because the water in the Napo comes from the melting snowcaps of Antisana and Cotopaxi. I don't mind climbing in snow,' grinned Jim. 'But I don't want to bathe in the stuff, even when it's newly melted!'

'Look up the cliff!' his friend said, pointing up the sheer face to where their home was. 'There can't be many houses with fifty-five mud steps between the bedroom and the bath!'

Jim decided that Pete needed his hair washed, and pushed him right down into the water.

Work was soon underway on an airstrip, with 40 or so men toiling on it each day. Jim and Pete spent their mornings on language study. Afternoons were much more physical.

'Time for my first machete practice,' Jim told his colleague.

The tree he hacked down didn't stand a chance, but it did throw a surprise at him.

'Aw,' Jim sighed, as a little baby bird fell from the tree. 'I'm sorry I've knocked you out your nest and chopped your home to the ground.'

Bending down, he picked the little creature up ... and nearly dropped it in suprise! It wasn't a bird, but a huge yellow caterpillar, with hair two inches long!

Soon people began beating a track to the missionaries' door for medical attention. Although Jim had begun to master the machete, the lad with the split head had not. And while Pete had blisters on his hands from working so hard, the man who arrived at their house with a broken arm was much more in need of attention.

The Quichua people took a little time to trust the two young men, but before long they decided that they were in Shandia to do them good.

'I just love these people,' Jim told Pete, after they had been in their new home for a while. 'They live so simply, yet they are content.'

'Sometimes they think we're stupid!' Pete commented.

Jim demanded to know when.

'Like when we collect our fruit and vegetables from the plane at Pano, then bring them home and soak them in potassium permanganate so that we can eat them raw.'

'We'd die of food poisoning otherwise!' laughed Jim.

'Or we could just shove everything in a pot and make it into soup like the Quichua do. We could have green soup on Mondays, yellow soup on Tuesdays and red soup on Wednesdays. That leaves blue, purple, orange and brown for the rest of the week.'

Jim grinned. 'I'll stick to my potassium permanganate soup and have at least some of my vegetables raw, thank you very much!'

'It would be much easier to visit the people if they lived in villages,' said Pete, as they walked together to visit some Quichua homes with Luis, their interpreter. 'Instead, they are strung all along the river, with some quite long distances between them.'

'There's one,' Jim pointed off to the right. 'And it looks identical to the last one, just a simple one-roomed house with palm thatch and split palm walls.'

'The children are coming to meet us,' Pete laughed. 'They are so cute!'

A boy and girl ran in their direction. They were short and stocky, with high cheekbones and thick jet-black hair. Their skin shone like polished bronze. Jim began to sing, and the children, whom he recognised from meetings they attended, joined in with him. The song Jim sang was in the Quichua language, which was what the children spoke. Pete and Jim, having learned Spanish, now had to begin to learn Quichua. Having Luis to translate from Spanish into Quichua meant that they could start telling the people about Jesus right away. But they knew that they could only use Luis for so long, and that they would have to master the language themselves.

'Do you realise what's happening?' Jim demanded, some time after starting work in Shandia.

'Which part of what's happening?' asked Pete.

'The people who attend mass in the Catholic Church are being given free insect repellent by the priest. Then they come to us for free medical care and boast about what the priest does for them. They're trying to wind us up!'

'Yea,' Pete agreed. 'And not only that. Some of their schoolboys are coming over here to eat our schoolboys' food, and even to sleep in their shelter!'

But their disappointment over that was forgotten the following morning when the first flight landed on the new Shandia airstrip.

'There must have been 150 Quichuas there!' Jim grinned, and they all heard the gospel! We have more to thank God for than just the airstrip!'

Soon afterwards their joy turned to sadness. Their cook's wife's baby died as it was being born. The infant would probably have survived had they taken advice from Dr Tidmarsh rather than from the 'knowing ones' – the Quichua witches and wizards. Jim took some slats from a wooden crate and made a tiny coffin. 'Life isn't very important here,' he wrote, 'and death even less. Nobody cried, for they don't regard as human a thing that has not breathed.' But from the tone of his notes, there was one person saddened at the baby's death, Jim Elliot himself.

That afternoon there was a fearful thunderstorm, and it lasted all of ten minutes. The ridge of the school roof blew off in the raging wind, and the clothes flew from the washing line and wrapped themselves round trees. Because there was no glass in their windows, piles of papers Jim and Pete had neatly stowed in their home, landed in a muddle all over the place. And Jim's heart was in a muddle too, as he had just heard on their short-wave radio that Elisabeth was leaving Quito for the western jungle. Would they ever be married? he wondered.

'Missionary life is certainly varied!' Jim laughed aloud.

Pete pretended to look surprised. 'I can't think what gives you that idea,' he said. 'All we've done today is study the Bible and pray, teach in the school as usual, show some boys the rudiments of volleyball, do some first aid on a couple of Indians who let a tree crash down on them, put out a minor fire caused by a kerosene lamp being knocked over, hack down a thorn bush to allow us to extend the garden in order to grow more vegetables, and help with some building work on the clinic. Apart from that we spoke to a group of men about the Lord, and visited a home where a family member has died, and told them about Jesus. I thought you said it was varied!'

The following morning, a messenger ran to Shandia and arrived breathless in front of Pete.

'Come. Help, please! A girl has been bitten by a snake!'

Pete yelled for his friend, and the pair of them grabbed their equipment and dashed to the river where the girl's father waited for them in his dugout. For 20 minutes he paddled upriver, before heading for the water's edge beside a small house. By then it was an hour since the girl had been bitten on the heel. No blood had come out of it at all which meant the venom was still in the child. Jim shoved a clean blade into his scalpel and slit the girl's heel once, twice and then a third time to make the blood flow freely.

'He's killing me!' the child cried. 'He's killing me!'

Knowing that he needed to wash the venom out with the child's flowing blood, Jim was about to cut a fourth time. But the family had gathered round when they heard the girl's screams, and he had to stop.

'Use the suction pump!' Pete said. 'Draw blood out that way!'

But the girl screamed all the louder, and they had to lay the pump aside.

Desperate to help, for the next hour Jim held the cuts open to allow the blood to flow, before giving his patient something to quieten her. Having done all they could for the girl, Pete and Jim packed up and left for home.

New Directions

Jim travelled to Quito in January 1953, and sent a telegram to Elisabeth to tell her that he was waiting for her there. Her journey to meet him was not an easy one. It involved a horseback ride, then ten hours in a banana truck that climbed 9,000 feet in that time! Jim took an engagement ring with him to Quito, and Elisabeth was very happy to accept it. When they separated, Jim did not go back to the jungle alone. His friend, Ed McCully — whom he had once thrown in the lake at Wheaton - had just arrived in Ecuador, and went with him for a trip to see his future home, for he and his wife were about to join Jim and Pete in their work. Before Ed left by plane from the Shandia airstrip ten days later, he and Jim planned buildings to develop the work there.

'It's wonderful even to know just enough Quichua to give a short talk now,' Jim said, six months after arriving in Shandia. 'But it's going to be a struggle to speak the language all the time at the Dos Rios Conference.'

Pete agreed. 'And because it's such a simplified language, it's not always easy to find words to explain things.'

'But we've got to keep trying,' Jim encouraged. 'We've just got to keep trying.'

The Dos Rios Conference in April 1953 was really hard work, especially as the preaching didn't seem to be making much of an impact. But as they were leaving, a little thing happened that really encouraged the missionaries.

'Goodbye, and God bless you all,' Jim said, as they walked down to the riverside, and their boat.

The Indian Christians went with them to see them off. Suddenly Jim was aware that two young girls had taken his hands. Serafina, who could not walk well, took one hand, and her friend, Christina, took the other.

'In every prayer we make we will pray for you,' the girls told Jim.

And there were many times in the future when Jim was to remember these girls and feel thankful for their prayers.

From the conference, Jim returned to Shandia to oversee the construction work that he and Ed McCully had planned together. But the rainy season set in with a furious storm. Jim's journal records the devastation.

'There have been several landslips. The generator is dangling on a rope over a sheer wall. The new house, once 30 yards from the cliff, is now a bare 15. The trail has completely gone. The river was frantic and huge – gnawing off great chunks of earth and stone and forest, and growling deep in its guts as it churned up the stones. It was a fearful thing to see.'

And the damage was not all done. Before the rain stopped, and the rivers receded to their normal height, their buildings at Shandia were swept away. The Indians helped Jim to save all they could. 'The first house went about 3.30 pm on Thursday,' he told Elisabeth, in a letter. 'The school went about midnight, and the school kitchen in the early hours of yesterday. The clinic and our Indian kitchen crashed down yesterday afternoon, and were washed away. Everyone is OK, but our little part of Shandia is no more. It has gone forever.'

Elisabeth, who was six hours walk away at Dos Rios, where she had begun her study of the Quichua language, set off for Shandia to do what she could to help. And the next few days were spent deep in mud searching for whatever could be saved.

'I can hardly wait for Ed to come,' Jim said, two weeks later. Then he thought sadly of Ed and Marilou's belongings that had come in advance of them, and that had been badly damaged in the floods. It was little wonder that Jim succumbed to a severe attack of malaria.

By August it seemed that the focus of their work would have to change, so Pete, Jim and Ed travelled on foot and by canoe along the Bobonaza River, looking for possible new mission stations. Elisabeth stayed behind to guard their muddied belongings.

'We met an amazing man,' Jim told her, on their return. 'His name is Atanasio. He has 15 children, and he has invited us to establish a school for them!'

'Where?' asked Elisabeth.

'At Puyupungu, where the Pastaze and Puyo rivers meet,' he explained. 'It's a wonderful opportunity as it usually takes time to be welcomed in a new area. We'd be welcome there right away.'

'Marilou and I need to learn some of the language first,' Ed McCully said. 'We couldn't go with you right away.'

Jim agreed. 'But where will you do that?'

'We should follow our original plan and stay around Shandia. We'll live in an Indian house for the time being.'

As each wondered what the next step should be, Jim realised that the time he had waited for had eventually come. 'How soon will you marry me?' he asked Elisabeth.

And they were married a few weeks later, in Quito, on 8th October 1953, Jim's 26th birthday.

Following their honeymoon, the Elliots flew with their belongings to Shell Mera, where they stayed overnight with Nate Saint and his wife, Marj, before Nate drove them to Puyo. Nate was the Missionary Aviation Fellowship pilot based at Shell Mera. From Puyo Jim and Elisabeth travelled by canoe to their new home at Puyupungu. Late that afternoon a welcome party paddled out to meet them. It was Atanasio and his friends! After sharing their first night in a house inhabited by many large cockroaches, Jim pitched the tent that was to be their home for the following five months. And for several weeks of that time Jim was very ill.

'Do you think you are fit to go to Shandia for Christmas?' Elisabeth asked her husband, after he was more or less better.

'Try to stop me!' Jim laughed. 'And we need time together with Ed and Marilou. Marj Saint says she'll meet us at Puyo and drive us to Shell Mera. Nate will fly us to Shandia from there.'

Elisabeth and Jim returned refreshed after their time away, and immediately started work on a house and airstrip at Puyupungu. By the end of March they were in their newly built home, and the airstrip was well on its way to completion. But much more important than that, some of the local people had put their trust in Jesus.

'Do you think we can leave Puyupungu so soon?' Elisabeth asked her husband, in May 1954, when he said they should move back to Shandia.

Jim nodded. 'Yes, I think we can, and we should. The school is up and running. We have young Christians growing here, and the house is finished and ready for missionaries to visit from time to time.'

'Not to mention that your dad is in Shandia helping to put up some mission buildings,' his wife grinned. 'And we wouldn't want to miss seeing him, would we?'

'No!' Jim laughed. 'We certainly would not!'

Leaving the people of Puyupungu in the Lord's care, the young couple closed up the house temporarily and went to Shandia, where they lived in a tiny house that Ed had built. The next few months were spent in serious construction work as a permanent mission station was erected.

'There are over 700 Indians here!' Marilou told Elisabeth, during the Young Men's Conference at Shandia, the following February. 'Some have come a long distance to be here.'

'It's just wonderful to see them sitting listening to the preaching,' Elisabeth agreed.

Pete Fleming had just arrived back from a visit to the States, having gone there to marry Olive. This was Olive's introduction to the work.

'Don't think there are always such large crowds,' Marilou cautioned her.

Olive smiled. 'It's OK,' she said. 'Pete has told me all about it, and I know this is extra special.'

It certainly was. Four young men were baptised, one of whom had been well known as a drunkard.

127

On Monday evenings there was a meeting for Christian believers at Shandia. No one taught at that meeting, rather those who trusted in Jesus sat and worshipped the Lord they loved. Sometimes an Indian or missionary would suggest a hymn they could sing together. Sometimes one of those present led in prayer. But much of the time was spent in the silent worship of God. Often the meeting ended with the singing of, 'kirikgunaga, kushiyanguichi – Cristo shamunmi!' which translates as 'Be happy, believers – Christ is coming!' Among those who gathered for these meetings were some young men Jim saw as potential leaders and teachers, and he set out to train them in the work.

In February 1955, Jim and Elisabeth went to Shell Mera, where he was to help to build a hospital. Elisabeth had something else on her mind as, two days after their arrival, she had a little daughter at the home of their friends, Nate and Marj Saint. The Elliots had discussed what they would call their child, but had not come to a firm conclusion. But no sooner was the little girl born, than Jim announced that her name was Valerie. And so it was. To add to Jim and Elisabeth's joy, Dad and Mum Elliot were at Shell Mera for their grand-daughter's birth.

'We have just learned of an Auca attack not far from Arajuno,' Jim wrote to his parents, soon after their return home to Portland. 'Although the house in Arajuno is ready for them, Ed is a little worried about going there with his family. The Aucas killed two children and their mother, and they were last seen heading up the Arajuno River in a stolen canoe. Please pray for Ed.'

While that concern was on their hearts, the young

128

missionaries were thrilled at God's goodness in their work among the Quichua people. In one week about 20 people became Christians in Dos Rios, around the same number in Pano, and a dozen in Shandia. Meanwhile Jim had things on his mind, practical things, like a construction project. Many a time he was grateful for what he learned when helping his brother, Bob, build his house! And his other brother, Bert, came to see how he was getting on with the hospital. He and his wife, who were missionaries in Peru, visited the Ecuadorian side of the family, where they met their new little niece, Valerie.

Grandparents always want to know what their grandchildren are doing, and Jim wrote interesting letters home.

'It's like hearing him speaking,' Mum Elliot said, when a letter arrived that autumn. 'Just listen to this.'

Dad Elliot settled with his cup of tea and listened.

'Valerie grows week by week,' his wife read. 'She is terrifically active, rolling about, and waving her legs as though she were cycling. Then she puts her hands over her head and whams them down again. Elisabeth has started giving her plantain flour, which she makes herself, and the little squirt loves it!'

'I can just picture her,' Dad Elliot laughed.

Mum Elliot poured herself a cup of tea and sat down.

'I'm so glad we went to see them,' she said. 'What a difference that makes! Now I can see in my mind's eye where they are and what they are doing.'

About the time that letter arrived in Portland, Oregon, the McCullys had some exciting news for their friends.

Ed and Nate had spotted some Auca houses just minutes' flying time away from Arajuno. Even the word Auca made something happen in Jim's heart. It was as though a seed had been planted there the first time he heard of the Auca people in Oklahoma in January 1950. Over the five-and-a-half years since then the seed had grown little by little. Prayer watered it, because Jim had not forgotten his longing to take the gospel to a people who had never heard the name of Jesus, and the Auca were just such a people. Might this be the opportunity he was waiting for?

The End and the New Beginning

'Tell us about your contact with the Auca people?' Jim said, excitement coursing through every part of him.

Ed began the story. 'Much of what we know of the people we learned from Dayuma, an Auca girl who fled as a teenager after a particularly cruel family feud. She told us that her people wear no clothes apart from vines tied tightly round their waist, ankles and wrists. Also both men and women have plugs of balsa wood – often an inch thick – through their earlobes. Dayuma wears her hair combed down over her ears to hide her Auca origins.'

'She has often been asked why her people kill so readily,' Nate said. 'But she is unable to give us an answer to that. All she says is that we should never trust them. They may appear friendly at first, but then they will turn round and kill.'

'After we moved to Arajuno,' continued Ed, 'we were very aware of the Auca, because one side of the river is Quichua territory, and the other side belongs to the Auca. Sometimes it didn't feel like a very safe place to be.'

'We noticed an Auca house as I was flying over the Arajuno,' Nate said. 'It's just a few minutes by plane from the McCullys' mission house.'

October 1955
Jim Elliot, Nate Saint, Ed McCully and a friend of theirs lay on the floor around a map of the area, working out how they could reach the Auca people.

131

'Whatever we decide, I think it's best that we keep it secret,' Ed suggested. 'Otherwise we'll have all sorts of people descending on us, from other missionaries to money-makers of all kinds.'

'Agreed,' said the others in unison.

That night plans began to be laid. But normal work had to go on, and for Jim that meant a concerted effort to train young Christians as church leaders and preachers.

'There have been new Auca attacks recently at the mouth of the Arajuno River,' Jim wrote, soon afterwards. 'Ed is alert and has an electric fence operating. On Tuesday I want to go over to meet Dayuma to learn some phrases in her own language. I also intend buying a pig for the schoolboys to raise.'

Before long, Jim was putting his newly-learned phrases to good use. He flew with Nate and Ed over the Auca settlement. Using a battery-operated loudspeaker he called down to the people in their own language, 'We are your friends.'

It was easy to be friendly with the Aucas at a height of 2000 feet, but the men in the plane knew that it would be more difficult at close range.

'Trade us a lance for a machete,' called Jim, through the speaker.

Below them they could see a man run into a house and return with a lance. Nate circled the plane carefully, and lowered a basket containing a machete. Would the man take it and send back the lance? But what came back was just a slashed end of line. They had taken both the machete and the basket that had been lowered down.

Having lowered their line several times, Jim spoke again through the loudspeaker.

'We like you,' he said. 'You will be given a pot.'

Then they dropped a pot, tied with yellow ribbons so that the people could find it. Inside the pot was a yellow shirt and beads.

'They've got it,' Ed said. 'Look! He's waving the shirt in the air!'

Having made what was possibly friendly contact, Nate flew along a section of the Curaray River looking for potential landing sites. But, on finding none, the three men decided that they'd have to send for Whittaker landing gear for the plane, and make their own airstrip when it arrived.

'You are so excited!' Elisabeth said, when Jim arrived home. 'I've never seen you so excited before.'

In her heart, she knew that this was it. For Jim, this was the mission of his life. Something in Elisabeth's mind began to niggle. Should they really leave the work at Shandia for this, a work that was going really well for … for what?

'Jim, are you sure you are supposed to go to the Aucas?' she asked her husband one day.

'I am called,' he replied.

Elisabeth's unsettlement left her. If Jim was called by God, it was fine. She was right behind him. In fact, she made a start on learning the Auca language, and found the work thrilling.

'Might we move to the Auca village after friendly contact is made?' Elisabeth wondered, aloud.

'That's in the future,' Jim said. 'The priority now is to find or build a landing strip. We've decided to go down the Curaray River in a canoe first to try to identify a suitable place.'

But the letter he wrote to his parents at that time didn't mention Operation Auca at all. When the men decided on secrecy, they kept to it. Instead, Jim wrote home about Valerie.

'She has taken to pulling herself to a standing position in her playpen and letting herself down again. You'd love her now. She's a regular giggling doll. She laughs a lot and looks like an Elliot. What in the world do people do who have triplets?'

While work went on as usual so far as anyone outside of the close-knit group knew, Operation Auca was also proceeding.

27th November 1955.

'Nate and I made my second Auca flight,' recorded Jim. 'We saw a woman wearing a garment that had been dropped earlier. One house has a model aeroplane carved on its upper ridge! And I saw a thing that thrilled me. It seemed an old man, who stood beside his house, waved with both arms as if to signal us to come down. Aucas waving us to come! Dropped several articles with streamers attached to help the people find them. They tied something to the line, but we lost it as we wound it in.'

Not long afterwards, Nate Saint found a beach on the Curaray River that he felt sure he would be able to land on. It seemed that face-to-face contact would take place very soon.

'What happens if you don't come back?' Elisabeth asked her husband.

'If God wants it that way, darling,' Jim replied, 'I am ready to die for the salvation of the Aucas.'

Despite his deep longing to tell the Auca people about Jesus, Jim still had other work to do. The Elliots were invited to spend part of December with the Flemings, who not long before moved to Puyupungu. They had arranged a fiesta, and Jim was their guest speaker.

An urgent radio message from Marilou in Arajuno, brought the little group's mind right back to the Auca.

'An Indian who was staying with us got up early and almost ran head-on into a naked Auca standing with a lance in his hand,' she said, sounding really scared. 'And it was less than 50 yards from our house.'

Ed and Nate flew out immediately, but they saw nothing of the man.

'Tell me exactly what happened,' Ed told his wife, when they had completed their search of the area.

She repeated what she'd said on the radio, and then told them that the Indian had wanted to kill the intruder, but she took his gun away and shouted, 'I like you' to the Auca, in his own language. But by then the man was out of sight.

The Flemings and Elliots went to Arajuno to be with Ed and Marilou for Christmas. No doubt Marilou was particularly glad of Elisabeth and Olive's company. She'd had a very frightening experience. Sitting round the little bamboo Christmas tree that their hostess had made, the missionary couples discussed Operation Auca, and prayed about contact being made on ground level. It was scheduled for the first week of January 1956, just a few short days away.

The team had grown by one, as Nate recruited Roger Youderian, a missionary to the Jívaros, who lived in the southern jungle.

On 28th December, Jim wrote home to his parents, telling them of Operation Auca for the very first time.

'By the time this reaches you, Ed and Pete and I and another fellow will have attempted with Nate a contact with the Aucas. We have prayed for this and prepared for several months, keeping the whole thing secret. Not even our nearby missionary friends know of it yet. ... I don't have to remind you that these are completely naked savages, who have never had any contact with white men other than killing them. They do not have firearms, but kill with long chonta-wood lances. They have no word for God in their language, only for devils and spirits.'

1956

Monday 2nd January

'The weather is so good,' Nate radioed to Jim, 'that I think I should shuttle you to Arajuno today rather that tomorrow.'

Elisabeth immediately began packing little gifts for the Aucas. By the time they reached the airstrip, the Missionary Aviation Fellowship plane was circling in to land. Jim kissed Elisabeth, hopped on board, and the plane took off. It took a few days to transfer all their equipment to Palm Beach on the Curaray River, and to get the five men there too.

Wednesday 4th January

'We had a good night,' Jim wrote. 'We didn't set a watch last night, as we really felt cosy and secure in our bunks in our hut 35 feet up a tree. We saw puma tracks on the beach and heard them last night. ... Our hopes are up but no signs of the "neighbours" yet. Perhaps today is the day the Aucas will be reached. It was a fight getting this hut 35 feet up the tree, but it is sure worth the effort to be off the ground.' Having slept well, the missionaries spent part of the next day walking around Palm Beach shouting out the Auca phrases they had learned from Dayuma.

Friday 6th January

Three Aucas appeared out of the jungle, two young women and a young man. After their initial surprise, the missionaries greeted their visitors with 'Puinanis,' which is 'Welcome' in their own language. In fact, they were welcomed over and over again with puinanis after puinanis! Jim stepped into the water to go towards them, and eventually accompanied them to their side of the river. The three young Aucas seemed so friendly that Nate took the man – they called him George – up in the plane, and showed him his home settlement from the air. One of the young women looked through the pages of a magazine, and the other rubbed her back against the fabric of the aeroplane. Eventually their visitors left, bearing gifts with them.

'Do you think they'll be back tomorrow?' was the subject for discussion as Jim, Roger and Ed settled down in their tree-house that night. Nate and Pete went the few minutes' flight back to Arajuno.

But Saturday came and brought no Aucas with it. Nate did a sortie over the houses and was disturbed to find signs of fear there. Some of the people ran into their homes when they saw the plane overhead. Having let down some gifts, Nate spotted 'George' among the men who went for them. That night, Nate and Pete slept at Arajuno.

Sunday 8th January

As the plane took off early in the morning, Pete looked back, and said, 'So long, girls. Pray. I believe today's the day.'

Marilou sent them off to Palm Beach with warm blueberry muffins and ice cream. No doubt the five young men enjoyed the treat.

'I think you should fly over the Auca village,' one of them suggested.

Nate went up alone, and saw only women and children near their homes.

'I guess that means the men are on their way,' Nate concluded. As he touched down, he yelled to his friends, 'This is it, guys! They're on the way!'

Nate told their wives in code what was happening when he radioed them at 12.30 pm. 'Looks like they'll be here for the early afternoon service. Pray for us,' he said. 'This is the day! Will contact you next at 4.30.'

At 4.30 that afternoon, five young wives listened to the sound of silence on their radio receivers. Within the hour, helicopters and planes were out in search of their husbands in the area of Palm Beach. It was a helicopter pilot who saw the first body, and the other four were found soon afterwards. All five had been brutally murdered. Nate Saint's watch had stopped at 3.12 pm. When Elisabeth Elliot, Marj Saint, Olive Fleming, Marilou McCully and Barbara Youderian heard the news, they had a message for the rescue services, and for all their families and friends, 'The Lord has closed our hearts to grief and hysteria, and filled them with his perfect peace.'

These five Christian women had peace in God's promise that those who love him are taken home to heaven when they die. Even in their sadness at losing their young husbands, they rejoiced that Jim, Nate, Pete, Ed and Roger had gone to their heavenly home, and that they were safe forever with Jesus.

Afterwards

January 1956
News of the martyrdom of the five missionaries soon spread throughout the world, and Christians gave thanks for their courage and determination to reach out to people who had never heard the name of Jesus. They also prayed for the young widows and their children.

8th October 1958
Elisabeth Elliot remained in Ecuador after Jim's death. Nineteen months later she took her little daughter, Valerie, and went with Rachel Saint (Nate's sister) to live and work among the Auca people. This was made possible through their friendship with Dayuma and two other young Auca women Elisabeth had befriended. Elisabeth and Valerie Elliot left that work in December 1961. By then they had seen many of the Auca people come to faith in the Lord Jesus Christ, even some of those who were involved in the murders at Palm Beach. The Elliots returned to the United States in 1963.

2000
Colombian born Renaldo Bernal, his wife Blanca, and their three-year-old son, Michael, watched as a Mission Aviation Fellowship plane came down to land at a new airstrip deep in the Ecuadorian jungle, the homeland of the Auca

– who by then were known as the Waorani people. The airstrip had been hacked out of the jungle by the Waorani using their machetes. This was the first of a dozen flights that would carry in bags of cement, fuel for chain saws, generators, cement posts, boxes of nails, and many other building materials unavailable in the jungle. The Bernals had worked with the Waorani for four years, and the cargo MAF was carrying in was the stuff of which their dreams were made. For they dreamed of a Bible College deep in the jungle, built by Waorani, a place where the Waorani would be trained to reach out to their own people with the good news that Jesus Christ saves sinners, even those who were involved in the killing of Jim Elliot, Nate Saint, Ed McCully, Pete Fleming and Roger Youderian at Palm Beach, on the Curaray River, on Sunday 8th January 1956.

Jim Elliot Time Line

October 8	1927	Jim Elliot is born in Portland, Oregon
	1928	First video recordings by John Logie Baird
	1929	Start of the Great Depression, U.S.A.
	1932	Parking Meter invented by Carl C Magee
	1933	Hitler becomes Chancellor of Germany
	1935	Ethiopia is invaded by Italy
	1937	Amelia Earhart disappears in the Pacific
	1938	Teflon developed by Roy Plunkett
	1939	World War II begins
	1941	Aerosol developed by Lyle David Goodloe
		Pearl Harbour attacked.
		U.S. enters World War II.
	1944	The first information-processing computer invented by Howard Aiken
	1945	Jim Elliot attends Wheaton College
		Atomic bomb developed by J Robert Oppenheimer
		World War II ends
	1946	Jim goes on mission trip to Mexico
	1947	Microwave oven invented by Percy Spencer
	1949	Mao Zedong declares The Communist People's Republic of China
	1950	Jim hears of Auca Indians for the first time
	1952	Jim and Pete Fleming arrive in Ecuador
		Elizabeth II ascends the British throne
	1953	The first Quichua Bible Conference
		Jim Elliot marries Elisabeth Howard
	1954	Segregation in U.S. schools is made illegal
	1955	Nate Saint and Ed McCully fly over Auca villages for the first time
		Valerie Elliot born
January 3	1956	The missionaries set up camp at Palm Beach
January 6	1956	Three Aucas spend day with the missionaries

January 8	1956	Last Radio contact
	1958	Dayuma, an Auca woman returns to her tribe to share her Christian faith
		Elisabeth and Valerie go to live amongst the Aucas or Waorani
	Today	Missionary work continues and many of the Waorani have become Christians.

Life Summary
JIM ELLIOT (1927-1956)

"He is no fool who gives what he cannot keep
to gain what he cannot lose."
(An entry in Jim Elliot's journal)

Jim Elliot is a Christian martyr from the twentieth century, one of many. He was killed, along with four others, at the hands of Auca Indians who are known today as the Waorani. Jim's story has become a legacy to the mission field in that countless young men and women have been inspired to missionary work through the message of his life and death. Jim's story has, without a doubt, been made known throughout the world primarily through the writing and speaking of his wife, Elisabeth.

Born in Portland, Oregon, Jim came from a family that had Scottish origins as well as links to agriculture and evangelism. He became a Christian as a six year old after attending a church meeting. His faith in Christ remained from that day the central part of his life.

After high school he enrolled in Wheaton College in 1945. One of the other students, five years his senior, was Billy Graham. Jim met his future wife, Elisabeth, at Wheaton. The following years would mould Jim academically as well as in his spiritual life. Amy Carmichael became one of his role models and heroines.

Graduating from Wheaton, the mission field that God called him to the unexplored frontiers of Ecuador in Latin America. Elisabeth came too, and after Jim's first year of work in Ecuador, they were married in 1953. Jim and four companions made it their personal mission to reach out beyond the limits of civilisation to spread the gospel even further afield. The young men flew their MAF Piper plane over the lands of the Auca tribe. Much planning and many preparatory flights took place over the preceding weeks but they had no idea what would face them on their first landing.

On 2nd January 1956, Nate Saint began to ferry his companions, Jim Elliot, Pete Fleming, Ed McCully, Roger Youderian, and their survival equipment to the planned landing spot. The aircraft, a Piper was ideally constructed, and had the ability to fly in circles at a low speed. It took many flights from the airstrip at Arajuno to 'Palm Beach' to ferry everyone and everything, but on the last flight, Nate circled low over the Waorani house before landing, to encourage them to come to visit them. Finally assembled at Palm Beach, the young men made a camp, with a tree house for extra security at night, and they settled down to wait.

They waited for three days, until on 6th January, three Waorani walked the four miles to the riverbank where the aeroplane had landed. After initial greetings one indicated, by drawing in the sand, that he wanted a ride in the plane, so Nate flew him over the Waorani house.

The following day two Warorani went home, but during conversation with other tribal members one lied about the missionaries' intentions and said that they had tried to kill them. As a result, five Waorani men plotted to kill the missionaries and proceeded to make spears. On the afternoon of the 8th January, the Indians attacked; the five missionaries were speared to death, and their bodies left by the river.

Jim Elliot left behind his wife Elisabeth and his daughter Valerie, who was only a baby at the time. The other missionaries left behind wives and children too. It was some time before the families knew what had happened, but they soon found themselves the centre of media and world attention.

Elisabeth continued Jim's work among the Waorani and, with her young daughter, accompanied a Waorani woman, Dayuma, to the tribal home to live with people who had killed her husband. Nate Saint's sister Rachel was also central to that work over the following years. Rachel lived and died there amongst the Waorani Indians. Nate Saint's son now works amongst the same people who killed his father.

This was accomplished through the profound and simple witness of a young widow and others who grieved, but who would not give in to vengeance. The Waorani saw Christ's love in action and as a result reached a turning point in their people's history.

ECUADOR INFORMATION

Located on the Northwest Coast of South America Ecuador lies in both the Northern and Southern Hemispheres, divided by the imaginary Equator line. It is bordered by Colombia to the north, Peru to the south and east and to the west by the Pacific. Though one of the smallest countries in South America, Ecuador is the most geographically, biologically, ethnically and culturally diverse country in the world.

Ecuador's continental territory is crossed from north to south by the Andes mountain range that divides it into three strongly distinct natural regions: the Coastal Region, the Inter-Andean Region and the Amazon Region. In addition to these regions Ecuador has a fourth region: the Galapagos, Islands located 1,000 kilometres from Ecuador's coastline. The topography of the country ranges from sea level up to over 6,000 metres at the Andean snowcaps, and the climate from tropical equatorial rainy weather to perpetual snow.

El Oro, Manabi and Los Rios provinces are the major agricultural areas, and are home to many fishing villages. The rest of the coastal areas have marshes, mangrove forests, tourist resorts and export ports.

BASIC FACTS

Official name: Republic of Ecuador.

Type of government: Democracy, Presidential Republic.

Capital city: Quito.

Main cities: Guayaquil, Quito, and Cuenca.

Currency: US Dollars.

Languages: Spanish (official) native languages i.e. Quichua (Incas' language) and Shuar.

Population: Approximately 13,600,000.

Highest point: Chimborazo Volcano, 6,300 metres. The highest active volcano in the world is the Ecuadorian Cotopaxi, reaching 5,897 metres.

Natural resources: Fish, timber, oil and mining.

CLIMATE

There are two main seasons: a wet season followed by a dry season. It is generally cooler in the Inter-Andean region and more tropical with humid, wetter climates in the Amazon and Coastal areas.

The Coastal Region lies west of the Andes towards the Pacific Ocean. Generally it has a tropical climate – hot and moist, averaging 25° C (76° F) to 31° C (90° F). However, the cold Humboldt current (that flows from Chile into Ecuador's warmer equatorial waters) modifies this heat and humidity.

Ecuador can also be effected by El Niño. This is a phenomenon which leads to torrential storms and flooding as huge amounts of water are scooped from the ocean and thrown onshore. As a result of the volcanoes and high mountain peaks there are varying mini-climates. For example, the valleys and hollows of the Andes are baking hot during the day but are much cooler in the evenings. In contrast, the southerly areas towards the Peruvian frontier enjoy more moderate temperatures.

ECOLOGY & ENVIRONMENT

The animal life of Ecuador is varied. Large mammals include the bear, jaguar and wildcat, and smaller mammals are the weasel, otter and skunk. Reptiles, including the lizard, snake, and crocodile, thrive on the slopes of the Andes and along the coastal lowlands. Birds are the most varied group, and many North American birds migrate to Ecuador during the northern winter.

The country of Ecuador, despite its small area, is the most biological diverse place on earth. The Eastern Oriente province has provides 10% of the world's total plant species. Around 15% of all protected and endangered bird species are only found in Ecuador. Of the 3000 species known throughout the world, 50% are represented in Ecuador, making it the densest bird population on the planet.

The Amazon Region begins to the East of the Andes. This region is characterized by its exuberant and unique rainforest ecosystems. High temperatures prevail, with abundant rainfall. The average temperature varies from 23° to 26 °C (72° to 80° F). The rivers formed in the mountains by the melting snow empty into the Amazon, Napo River is the longest in Ecuador and flows for 530 miles.

ECONOMY

Ecuador is the premier exporter of bananas to the entire world, and is also an important shrimp farming area. In addition it is a major exporter of tuna, sardine and white fish. The country's main export is petroleum. Ecuador's major agriculture products are coffee, bananas, rice, potatoes, cacao (from cacao beans used in chocolate production), manioc, sugarcane, plantains, cattle, pigs, sheep, beef, pork, shrimp, balsa wood, dairy products and fish.

GALAPAGOS
ISLANDS

COLOMBIA

EQUATOR

Esmeraldas

Quito

Cotopaxi

PACIFIC
OCEAN

Chimborazo

Shell

AMAZON
BASIN

Napo

Cononaco

Tigre

Pastaza

Guayaquil

ECUADOR

PERU

Golf of
Guayaquil

Santiago

PERU

NORTH
AMERICA

GUYANA

VENEZUELA

SURINAME

FRENCH GUIANA
(France)

COLOMBIA

ECUADOR

Equator

GALAPAGOS IS.
(Ecuador)

Amazon R.

PERU

BRAZIL

Pacific
Ocean

BOLIVIA

**SOUTH
AMERICA**

PARAGUAY

URUGUAY

CHILE

ARGENTINA

Atlantic Ocean

FALKLAND IS.
(U.K.)

Margaret Wilson: Danger on the Hill
by Catherine Mackenzie

Margaret Wilson is one of the Covenanters, a group of people who are being persecuted by the Soldiers of the King. All they want to do is to worship God in freedom but that is not allowed. Margaret and her family live in fear of their lives so together with her brother and sister they leave the family home to live in hiding in the hills. How do they survive? Will the soldiers find them? And who is the young man who promises to help them find shelter through the long cold, winter months?

Margaret has to learn to trust her friends and her family but most importantly she learns to trust in God and his care for her. This is a trust that remains with her even when things go wrong. There may be danger on the hill and Margaret's life may hang by a thread but she knows that she has a great and faithful God that she can trust, whatever happens.

ISBN: 185792-7842

INSPIRING STORIES OF CHRISTIAN MARTYRS

William Tyndale: The Smuggler's Flame
by Lori Rich

William Tyndale was an educated and accomplished young man but his greatest accomplishment was never recognised by the mighty men and rulers of his day. His last prayer was 'Oh Lord, open the King of England's eyes.' For it was that King with others who harried him across Europe in order to put a stop to the translation work on the English Bible.

William believed that the people of his own land should be allowed to read God's word in their own language. However the rulers of the churches and the thrones of Europe feared for their own influence and power. God's word translated for the ordinary people would bring them down. So instead they went all out to bring William Tyndale down before he could do any further damage. However this was not to be - even as he was burnt at the stake Tyndale had already translated most of the Bible into English and his work was done.

ISBN: 1 85792 9721

INSPIRING STORIES OF CHRISTIAN MARTYRS

Polycarp: The Crown of Fire
by William Chad Newsom

Polycarp was one of the leaders of the early church during a time when persecution was what the believers expected and martyrdom was honoured. Many people suffered under the tyranny of Rome and died as a result of torture, beatings or the Roman public's unquenching desire for amusement.

In this book you can accompany Polycarp and his companions as they face these crowds and their Roman enemy in order to pass on the legacy of truth. To gain the Crown of Fire Polycarp must be willing to suffer for Christ. But will his courage hold? What does the Crown of Fire really mean? Is it right to fight or should the Christians just give in? What does God want Polycarp, the Bishop of Smyrna, to do?

Timeline and other facts about the Early church appear in this book.

ISBN: 1 84550 0415

INSPIRING STORIES OF CHRISTIAN MARTYRS

Rainforest Adventures
Amazon Adventures
by Horace Banner

The animals and plants of the Rainforest and Amazon river are fascinating examples of God's marvellous creation. But what else can we learn from these animals? There are many ways that these creatures point us to our great God and creator. If you feel like an adventure but can't afford the plane ticket, if you just want to find out more about God's amazing world jump into these books. You'll enjoy them and you'll also find out more about what it's really like to be a pioneer missionary in South America.

Rainforest Adventures: ISBN: 185792 6277
Amazon Adventures: ISBN: 185792 4401

AMAZING STORIES OF NATURE AND WILD LIFE

Missionary Stories
from around the World
by Betty Swinford

Have you ever wanted to travel the world? Many people have
done just that in order to bring the good news of Jesus Christ
to people who have never been taught about his love This
book introduces us to some very adventurous missionaries as
well as some of the unsung heroes from behind the scenes.
Not everyone gets on plane or a boat to bring Jesus to other
lands. Some people reach out ot their own people, on their
own streets and some people are the supporters of those
missionaries who chose to leave their homes. People who
travel, people who stay at home, people who pray - they are
all part of God's missionary work. This book gives you danger,
excitement and adventure all through working for God.

ISBN: 1 84550 0423

MISSIONARY ADVENTURE STORIES

Staying Faithful - Reaching Out!

Christian Focus Publications publishes books for adults and children under its three main imprints: Christian Focus, Mentor and Christian Heritage. Our books reflect that God's word is reliable and Jesus is the way to know him, and live for ever with him.

Our children's publication list includes a Sunday school curriculum that covers pre-school to early teens; puzzle and activity books. We also publish personal and family devotional titles, biographies and inspirational stories that children will love.

If you are looking for quality Bible teaching for children then we have an excellent range of Bible story and age specific theological books.

From pre-school to teenage fiction, we have it covered!

Find us at our web page:
www.christianfocus.com